WRITING AND
EDITING ACTIVITIES

Aaron Perkus
Norwalk Community College

THE COLLEGE WRITER'S REFERENCE

FOURTH EDITION

Toby Fulwiler
University of Vermont

Alan R. Hayakawa
The Patriot News

Upper Saddle River, New Jersey 07458

PEARSON
Prentice
Hall

© 2005 by PEARSON EDUCATION, INC.
Upper Saddle River, New Jersey 07458

10 9 8 7 6 5 4 3 2 1

ISBN 0-13-189604-0

Printed in the United States of America

Contents

A NOTE TO STUDENTS:

The activities in this booklet have been numbered to coordinate with the chapters of The College Writer's Reference, Fourth Edition. The numbers and section letters provided in parentheses (12a or 25e, for example) point to corresponding topic discussions in the handbook for help in completing the activities.

Voice and Tone

Activity 1-1

Maintaining tone (See 1d.)

Edit the following passage from a literary analysis to maintain an appropriate academic tone. More than one edited version is possible.

It's wild how completely different the three main characters in Tennessee Williams's Streetcar Named Desire are from each other. First, you have Blanche. She's this hard-nosed Southern belle who pretends to be all delicate and helpless, but really she's a major control freak who's always ordering everybody around and making a big deal to get her own way. You feel sorry for her sometimes, but she gets on your nerves too. The play begins when Blanche crashes with her baby sister, Stella, and her sister's husband, Stanley. Now, Stella is this sweet, basic sort of person. (How did these two ever get to be sisters?) She'd like to tell Blanche where to get off, but she just doesn't have the guts. So Blanche moves in, and then things get sort of hairy. Stanley is this dumb, low-class kind of guy with no manners but lots of macho. He and Blanche just don't hit it off at all: he thinks she's a lying witch, and she thinks he's an animal. At the same time, though, she's very flirty with him, which doesn't help matters. Sweet little Stella, of course, is right in the middle, having to defend Stanley to Blanche and Blanche to Stanley. You just have this foreboding that the situation is going to become volatile.

Activity 1-2

Achieving the right level of formality (See 1d.)

Edit the following two paragraphs, adjusting the tone to the appropriate level of formality. The first paragraph is from a paper relating a personal experience; the second is from a formal research paper. More than one edited version of each paragraph is possible. For help, see box on p. 9 of *CWR*.

Personal Experience Essay

Who would find it credible that two adults would have trouble convincing one eight-pound feline that the time had come for his annual physical examination? Upon spotting his cage, the cat exits the room as quickly as he can. Under the bed, over the bed, up the staircase, down the staircase, he rushes with extreme celerity from one room to the next, ever eluding our grasp. When his outrageous behavior ceases, and we have him cornered, I stealthily approach him and apprehend him. I loudly proclaim myself triumphant as I deposit him in his place of confinement and secure the top.

Formal Research Paper

At the Dryden Correctional Center, the guys who run the education department try to prepare the inmates for living on the outside. That way criminals won't (they hope!) turn back to a life of crime. OK. Sounds like a good idea. But how do they do it? Well they make sure that as soon as the criminals get tossed in the slammer they start getting an education. This is so that they will have a better chance of getting jobs when they get out. The way they figure it is if the criminals get jobs, they won't have to turn to crime to make money. The educational programs are completely voluntary. Lots of the inmates take them, though.

Activity 1-3

Maintaining consistency (See 1d.)

Edit the following passage from a formal research essay, removing any inappropriate shifts in tone. More than one edited version is possible. For help, see box on p. 9 of *CWR*.

Whenever a new movie geared toward young children is being readied for release, a multiplicity of promotional advertising ensues. First, the movie receives advanced publicity through endless television exposure. TV commercials promoting the movie are sandwiched between kids' favorite cartoon shows on their favorite cartoon network. Next, the movie gains added exposure through its own sweepstakes where children can win movie merchandise and the chance to see the world premiere. Then along come the cheesy toys such as action figures from the movie that can be yours just by downing a meal at a fast food chain. Of course, parents know the drill: they must buy at least 10 happy meals to get all six of the action figures. The come on doesn't stop there because the movie producers stick it to parents again when they release the collector's edition of the movie, which just appeared in theaters less than a year ago.

Activity 1-4

Maintaining consistency (See 1d.)

Edit the following passage from a formal argumentative essay, making sure to maintain a consistent, appropriate tone. More than one edited version is possible.

You can really see the similarities between Shakespeare's King Lear and Jane Smiley's novel A Thousand Acres. Smiley makes you think of Shakespeare's play on purpose, and she expects you to be with it enough to catch on. You can see the parallels even in the names she gives to her characters. The three sisters in A Thousand Acres are named Ginny, Rose, and Caroline. These names make you think of Lear's daughters, Goneril, Regan, and Cordelia. Get it? (The first letters are the same.) In both the play and the novel, one really important idea is how parents and kids get along. In Smiley's story, Caroline, the youngest daughter, doesn't like her father's plan to retire and divide his huge farm among his three daughters, so he chills her. In King Lear, Cordelia, also the youngest, won't compete with her sisters in telling her old dad how crazy about him she is just so she can get the largest part of his kingdom. In both works, the two older sisters tell their dad what he wants to hear, but the youngest stands up to him.

Prewriting

Activity 3-1

Brainstorming exercises (See 3a.)

Brainstorming is a type of private freewriting designed to generate ideas quickly and reveal interesting associations writers may have among topics. It is often the case that surprising ideas emerge when students trust in this process. For example, consider the following brainstorm:

Ideas for my next paper:
Chess
Mowing the lawn
Arsenic leaching from pressure treated lumber
Vaccines and autism (myth or science?)
Summer vacation
Driving to work or school
Movies I want to see
Friendship
What are the elements of good leadership?
Athletes breaking the law
Why is *American Idol* so popular?

Look through this list and pick one to make your own. Write a paragraph about it, trying to bring in descriptive writing and specific details from your own experience. Now generate your own list, circle the entry that most surprised you, and write a paragraph about it. Chances are there is some excellent writing waiting to be unleashed.

Activity 3-2

Looping in Action (See 3b.)

Looping is a form of freewriting designed to draw the writer deeper into the material by "looping" back and re-exploring material that emerges from the initial freewrite. Look at the following freewrite (and notice that it is full of grammatical blunders—that is part of the freedom!) and circle the sentence that most interests you. Write that sentence on the top of a fresh piece of paper and freewrite for five minutes using the initial sentence as a springboard to get you started. After five minutes, repeat the process by picking a sentence from your own new writing, copy it onto a new page, and begin again.

The freewrite:

I have been an active Survivor fan ever since the show first opened about five years ago; however, I think it is going in the wrong direction lately. This recent idea of having the public vote for their favorite Survivor, so he or she could win a million dollars, is really sounding too much like American Idol. After all, should the viewers be able to totally control who wins? It gives the illusion of power while providing very bland entertainment. In fact, it is sort of like our political system—we get to vote, and someone wins, but are we really connected to the process, or is it just a kind of ritual to keep our attention? Next step will be to have all the reality programs viewer based—perhaps the already are. Imagine Donald Trump hiring whoever had the most votes, or Joe Millionaire marrying based on voting results. What if we lived our lives that way—basing major decisions on popular opinion and poll results. Politicians get accused of doing that all the time, and perhaps it is normal to want to please people, but isn't there a tacit belief that to be human one must have the capacity of being unpredictable?

Activity 3-3
    Using clustering (See 3c.)

        Clustering is a prewriting strategy much like brainstorming and freewriting, but the idea is to create a non-linear map of ideas stemming from an original main topic. Look at the sample below, and draw the lines that you feel demonstrate the center idea with the logical off-shoots.

Arguing Positions

Activity 8-1

Taking a position (See 8a.)

For each of the following topics, state the issue (worded as a question) and then both a pro and a con position on the topic (written as statements).

1. euthanasia
2. death penalty
3. gun control
4. abortion
5. censorship
6. legalization of marijuana
7. driving age
8. legal drinking age
9. electoral college
10. the Patriot Act
11. electronic voting machines
12. animal experimentation for medical purposes
13. the Endangered Species Act
14. the environment
15. mandatory health care for all Americans
16. violence on television
17. reality T.V.
18. *American Idol*
19. reinstating the military draft
20. No Child Left Behind Act

Activity 8-2

Assembling Evidence (See 8c.)

For each of the following claims, generate ideas on how one could use all of the various type of evidence (facts, examples, inferences, expert opinion, personal experience) to support that claim.

1. Barry Bonds is the greatest baseball player of all time.
2. The correct use of seatbelts is tremendously important in saving lives.
3. On-line courses are better than traditional courses.
4. College aged students should never expect to do better than their parents did financially.
5. Divorce has long-term detrimental effects on the children.

Revising

Activity 9-1
Focused revising strategies (See 9b.)

The following is a WRITE draft. After you have read it, please pick one idea from the passage and write another draft that LIMITS the topic to only one idea, time or place.

People are always assuming that it is easy to win the Triple Crown. After all, if a horse wins the first two legs of the crown, the Derby and Preakness, the assumption is that this horse is clearly the best horse in the pack and should win every race. Not so fast. Horse-racing is a very difficult sport because there are two living, breathing creatures, the jockey and the horse, thus there are a myriad of factors that come into place each time a race occurs. Not to mention the crowd, the track conditions, the media; the pressure, the ability of the trainer, the health and well-being of the animal at the time of the race, the familiarity of the horse and jockey with the race and the distance, the weather conditions, the other horses in the race and the degree to which the other jockeys might be trying to do a kamikaze run to force the lead horse to mess up. Basically, this is what happened with Smarty Jones. While he may have been the best horse, he lost to the long-shot BirdStone. Why? There are many theories, ranging from the horse being over-rated in the first place to the jockey running him too hard too soon. Ultimately, it just wasn't meant to be. After all, Triple Crowns, whether in racing or in baseball, are incredibly rare although for different reasons. Perhaps the fact that in the 70's there were three Triple Crown winners created the illusion that it would happen all the time, and we haven't seen one since.

Activity 9-2
Focused revising strategies (See 9b.)

The following is a WRITE draft of an essay. Revise it to ADD research pertaining to past Triple Crown winners, interviews with the jockeys and trainers, or descriptions of what it looked like to watch the race.

People are always assuming that it is easy to win the Triple Crown. After all, if a horse wins the first two legs of the crown, the Derby and Preakness, the assumption is that this horse is clearly the best horse in the pack and should win every race. Not so fast. Horse-racing is a very difficult sport because there are two living, breathing creatures, the jockey and the horse, thus there are a myriad of factors that come into place each time a race occurs. Not to mention the crowd, the track conditions, the media, the pressure, the ability of the trainer, the health and well-being of the animal at the time of the race, the familiarity of the horse and jockey with the race and the distance, the weather conditions, the other horses in the race and the degree to which the other jockeys might be trying to do a kamikaze run to force the lead horse to mess up. Basically, this is what happened with Smarty Jones. While he may have been the best horse, he lost to the long-shot BirdStone. Why? There are many theories, ranging from the horse being over-rated in the first place to the jockey running him too hard too soon. Ultimately, it just wasn't meant to be. After all, Triple Crowns, whether in racing or in baseball, are incredibly rare although for different reasons. Perhaps the fact that in the 70's there were three Triple Crown winners created the illusion that it would happen all the time, and we haven't seen one since.

Activity 9-3
Focused revising strategies (See 9b.)

The following is a WRITE draft of an essay. Revise it to SWITCH point of view. Consider the following perspectives, and tell the story from their perspectives:

1. The losing jockey
2. The winning jockey
3. The fan who lost $1000 betting on the favorite
4. The child who watched horse-racing for the first time
5. The PETA (People for the Ethical Treatment of Animals) representative protesting the race

People are always assuming that it is easy to win the Triple Crown. After all, if a horse wins the first two legs of the crown, the Derby and Preakness, the assumption is that this horse is clearly the best horse in the pack and should win every race. Not so fast. Horse-racing is a very difficult sport because there are two living, breathing creatures, the jockey and the horse, thus there are a myriad of factors that come into place each time a race occurs. Not to mention the crowd, the track conditions, the media, the pressure, the ability of the trainer, the health and well-being of the animal at the time of the race, the familiarity of the horse and jockey with the race and the distance, the weather conditions, the other horses in the race and the degree to which the other jockeys might be trying to do a kamikaze run to force the lead horse to mess up. Basically, this is what happened with Smarty Jones. While he may have been the best horse, he lost to the long-shot BirdStone. Why? There are many theories, ranging from the horse being over-rated in the first place to the jockey running him too hard too soon. Ultimately, it just wasn't meant to be. After all, Triple Crowns, whether in racing or in baseball, are incredibly rare although for different reasons. Perhaps the fact that in the 70's there were three Triple Crown winners created the illusion that it would happen all the time, and we haven't seen one since.

Activity 9-4

Focused revising strategies (See 9b.)

The following is a WRITE draft of an essay. TRANSFORM it into a scene from a screenplay about the Philadelphia Farm that suddenly was competing for the coveted Triple Crown. What would be the background music? What would the shots look like? How would you present the owners and media?

People are always assuming that it is easy to win the Triple Crown. After all, if a horse wins the first two legs of the crown, the Derby and Preakness, the assumption is that this horse is clearly the best horse in the pack and should win every race. Not so fast. Horse-racing is a very difficult sport because there are two living, breathing creatures, the jockey and the horse, thus there are a myriad of factors that come into place each time a race occurs. Not to mention the crowd, the track conditions, the media, the pressure, the ability of the trainer, the health and well-being of the animal at the time of the race, the familiarity of the horse and jockey with the race and the distance, the weather conditions, the other horses in the race and the degree to which the other jockeys might be trying to do a kamikaze run to force the lead horse to mess up. Basically, this is what happened with Smarty Jones. While he may have been the best horse, he lost to the long-shot BirdStone. Why? There are many theories, ranging from the horse being over-rated in the first place to the jockey running him too hard too soon. Ultimately, it just wasn't meant to be. After all, Triple Crowns, whether in racing or in baseball, are incredibly rare although for different reasons. Perhaps the fact that in the 70's there were three Triple Crown winners created the illusion that it would happen all the time, and we haven't seen one since.

Document Design

Activity 17-1

Using Lists and Charts (See 17b.)

Take the following information and place it into an appropriately designed list and into an appropriately designed chart.

According to Forbes magazine, the most expensive houses in the U.S. are in the following places: Palm Beach-1 ($75 million), New York City ($62 million), Nantucket, MA ($54 million), Wainscott, NY ($50 million), Los Angeles ($45 million), Medina, WA ($45 million), Dallas, TX ($44.9 million), and Palm Beach-2 ($39 million).

Activity 18-1

Following Web page design guidelines (see 18b.)

For each of the two Web page links, arrange menu items in an order that reflects good design principles. For help, see box on p. 125 of *CWR*.

PBS Homepage (www.pbs.org):

TV Schedules, Programs A-Z, Search, Shop, Station Finders

U.S. Department of Education Homepage (www.ed.gov):

Contact Us, Directions, FAQs, Search, Site Map, Welcome, Topics A-Z

Activity 19-1

Creating a story portfolio (See 19b.)

Using the information provided below, construct one page that would be included in a student's story portfolio. Remember to use the principles of document design, particularly indentation, lists, and white space.

Molly was a student in a first-year composition class. She and her classmates read several narrative essays and then were asked to write their own personal narrative papers. In addition, they were to keep a journal in which they recorded their reactions to the readings and their own writing. Below is enough information for you to write in the first person as Molly. Remember that you can't include all the information, so pick and choose the most relevant details to make your point.

Essays that the class read: E. B. White's "Once More to the Lake," Langston Hughes' "Salvation," George Orwell's "Shooting an Elephant," and Loren Eiseley's "The Brown Wasps."

Journal entries:

9/4   I guess I just don't understand why anyone would do something they didn't believe in. I could sympathize with the young boy in "Salvation," because he was young and didn't know any better. But the guy in "Shooting an Elephant," he shouldn't have killed the elephant just because he didn't want to look like a fool. I know I wouldn't have.

9/6   O.K. so after discussing all the essays in class today I kind of understand why a person could possibly be pressured into doing something she didn't want to. So many of my classmates could relate to those essays, and they were willing to tell about their experiences to the class. It got me thinking about my own experiences with peer pressure and made me realize that I have done things that I wasn't so proud of, and I did them just to save face. I think I'll write about one of those experiences.

9/7   How did Hughes and Orwell do it—I mean write a personal essay that didn't seem cheesy. I'm having a heck of a time. I do remember that we discussed using detail that would show pressure instead of just telling the reader about it. Maybe I'll try that.

 Molly wrote about using her father's car without permission. Her three closest friends wanted to go to a party, but none of them could drive. She managed to use the car without her father ever finding out. Rather than telling the story as it unfolded, Molly chose to offer details about her father and how he had always demonstrated trust in her and contrast those details with the details of her friends' actions at the party.

Paragraph Structure

Activity 21-1

Creating Unified Paragraphs (see 21a.)

Edit the following paragraph to make it unified, well organized, and coherent, by eliminating any extraneous sentences, shifting and combining sentences so the ideas flow more logically, and adding transitional expressions to connect ideas. You may wish to divide this into more than one paragraph. More than one edited version is possible.

The Vietnam Veterans Memorial in Washington, D.C., was dedicated in 1982. It is another example of a work of public art that caused an outcry. Now it is recognized as a moving tribute to the soldiers who died fighting in Vietnam. When the original design was adopted, many veterans' groups were angry and critical. The monument consists of a seamless black marble slab that extends for several hundred yards, carved with the names of those who died, according to their date of death. At either end, the monument is only a few feet high, reflecting the lower number of casualties at the beginning and end of the war. From each end, visitors follow a path downward, and the dark monument gradually increases in height so that at its center it blocks everything from view except the rows of names of the dead. Visitors can locate the names they are looking for by consulting a booklet prepared by the Park Service. Early critics felt that the monument would appear negative and demeaning to those who died in Vietnam and insisted that a more conventional statue depicting heroic soldiers in combat be erected adjacent to the monument. Very few people spend much time looking at this statue. The monument is now perceived as a superior piece of public art. Family members and friends come back many times to touch the names of their loved ones, to leave messages and flowers, and to weep quietly for those who died in a controversial war.

Activity 21-2

Ensuring that paragraphs are unified (See 21a.)

Strengthen the following paragraphs by editing to ensure unity.

A. College radio stations do not receive lavish gifts, but they are not neglected in the grand sweep of promotions that back college-targeted records. The station I worked at has received everything from posters to gold records to bottles of liquor. Whether the promotions actually get records played is hard to document. The most common gifts are passes to performances and free copies of records.

B. The idea of planning seems simple enough. Communities are asked to designate areas for specific purposes, such as commercial, residential, or industrial use. The state's new requirement that every city and township formulate a plan may create a shortage of planners. Trying to pinpoint exactly what a planner does is a little more complicated.

Activity 21-3

Ensuring that paragraphs are well organized (See 21b.)

Strengthen the following paragraphs by editing to improve organization.

A.   The machine sucks the milk out of the cows with a vacuum. The vacuum pulsates so that the cows' teats won't lose circulation. Eight cows were lined up in the milking parlor, chewing their cuds and waiting to be mechanically milked. The workers put a black rubber tube over each teat on each cow's udder and turned on the milking machine. The milk flows through clear plastic hoses into glass jars and is siphoned from there into a tank.

B.   After the state legislature passed the Interstate Banking Act of 1987, First State Bank approached state regulators with a plan to merge with the Bank of the Ozarks. Interstate banking is new to the banking industry. Legislation passed before the Great Depression barred interstate banking in an effort to reduce the potential of bank failures and focus banks' investments on their own communities. Given that history, a merger plan like First State's should be evaluated for its effects on local communities and on the stability of the newly created bank.

Activity 21-4

Ensuring that paragraphs are coherent (See 21c.)

Strengthen the following paragraph by editing to improve coherence. Consider the use of transitional expressions, the order of sentences, and the use of repetition. More than one edited version is possible.

Each year thousands of college students from across the country use Spring Break as a time to escape the rigors of exams, research papers, and hard-nosed professors. They descend on the beaches of Florida, Texas, and even Mexico to frolic in the sun and drink lots of alcohol. Other students go to Mississippi, North Carolina, and Arkansas to help build low-income housing for Habitat for Humanity. They drive nails, paint houses, and remove trash. Rosie Click, a senior at St. Mary's College of Maryland, says, "For the three years, I've been telling myself that I should take my Spring Break at the beach, but I keep coming back to help out with Habitat for Humanity. I've never regretted it." "Some students just feel the need to help others," according to one college supervisor.

Activity 21-5

Ensuring that paragraphs are coherent (See 21c.)

Strengthen the following passage by editing to improve its coherence. More than one edited version is possible.

The zoning board rejected the proposal. The plan was the subject of three evenings of raucous debate. Then the city council took it up on appeal. The disagreement continued there for months. Some members said their first responsibility was to promote economic development in any form. The debate on the council reflected the divisions in the community. Growth should be regulated so that it does not harm existing businesses or the city as a whole, others believed. The project was approved two weeks after the new mayor took office. Amanda Robbins campaigned for mayor by rallying downtown businesspeople, historic preservationists, and neighborhood activists against the mall. Council member Steven McMillan ran on a pro-development, pro-mall platform. Both candidates said they wanted voters to end the deadlock on the proposal. The election was won by McMillan.

Strong Openings and Thoughtful Closings

Activity 22-1

Revising openings and closings

Following are the opening and closing paragraphs from a draft of a paper about the difficulties that recent college graduates are having finding suitable jobs. Edit each paragraph to make it more direct and engaging and to sharpen its focus. More than one edited version is possible.

As everybody knows, today we live in a very competitive society. Jobs are harder to find than they were ten years ago, especially for young people just entering the work force. The American dream of success seems to have died. For example, my brother graduated from college with a degree in marketing. He had a high average and many good recommendations from his professors. Yet, after two years, he is still looking for a job in his field. Working as an assistant manager in a hardware store, he can barely make his student loan and car payments, let alone afford rent, so he is still living at home with our parents.

In conclusion, I would like to say that I think it is everyone's responsibility to see that recent college graduates have a better chance. In my opinion, colleges should provide better career counseling, and more businesses should provide training opportunities. I think a voluntary program that would let students work off college loans through government-supported jobs is a good idea. Also, students need to do more career-related planning throughout their four years in school.

Activity 22-2

Making openings engaging (See 22a.)

Edit the following opening paragraph to make it more engaging. More than one edited version is possible.

Dr. Ravi Batra, an economist at Southern Methodist University, has described a long-term cycle of economic indicators. Those indicators, he believes, forecast a depression in the next few years. The World Futurist Society also predicts a global economic collapse rivaling the Great Depression of the 1930s. Both predictions cite the rash of bank failures in recent years, implying that the first indication of wider economic troubles will be the downfall of financial institutions.

Activity 22-3

Strengthening weak openings (See 22a.)

Edit the following opening paragraph to strengthen it. More than one edited version is possible. For help, see box on p. 153 of *CWR*.

Our society today faces many problems. One of these problems is increasing violence in schools. It seems that every time you turn on the news or pick up a newspaper, you read about another school shooting. Usually, the students committing the violence are shunned within their school, are bullied and teased by other students, and sometimes express their desire to exact revenge. In fact, I knew one schoolmate of mine who told me that he wanted to shoot a group of my classmates. But, I didn't feel that I could tell this to anyone at the school. I think if parents, teachers, school administrators, and students could provide a safe way to report this kind of information, we might be able to lessen the possibility of violence happening.

Activity 23-1

Making conclusions satisfying (See 23b.)

Edit the following conclusion to make it more satisfying. More than one edited version is possible.

Computers have radically altered our society and will undoubtedly continue to do so. But how far will computers take us? Will we like our destination? From the banking and finance industries to recreation and art, every aspect of our lives has been affected by the ramifications of RAM and ROM. Much as the Industrial Revolution and the Agricultural Revolution did in past centuries the Computer Revolution will fundamentally transform our culture in ways we cannot yet imagine. The three distinctive characteristics of computer transactions—speed of computation, ease of replication, and access through networking—are unremarkable in themselves, but when combined they change the very nature of information, the currency of our culture. No longer is knowledge accumulated over the centuries, unalterably fixed on pieces of paper, and painstakingly consulted when needed. Today's information resembles a rushing torrent always changing, impossible to contain or chart, and ready to sweep aside all limits or restrictions.

Activity 23-2

Strengthening weak conclusions (See 23a–e.)

Edit the following conclusion to strengthen it. More than one edited version is possible. For help, see box on p. 155 of *CWR*.

If the fighting ceases, parents can begin to talk to their children about the divorce and why it happened. From such discussions, children may learn that marriage is not something to rush into, which can be a good thing to learn. As they grow older, the emotional scar they will carry is knowing that their parents did not have a happy marriage, but I think that can be a good thing as well as a painful one.

Powerful Sentences

Activity 24-1

Strengthening sentence structure (See 24a-f.)

Edit the following paragraph to strengthen sentence structure. Use coordination and subordination to relate ideas, eliminate any overuse of coordination and subordination, and create parallelism where it is effective. More than one edited version is possible.

Some communities have succeeded in banning pornography completely. They have been able to close down businesses even when there was no chance of the X-rated materials falling into the hands of minors, and the town of Venice in Florida is a good example. A video store owner there kept X-rated videos in a separate locked room. Customers for these videos had to ask at the counter for a special key, and they had to present three forms of identification, and they also had to sign a special consent form, but some conservative members of the community learned about the business, and they were outraged and notified town officials. Police investigated the reports. Two days later the shop closed down. The owner chose not to challenge the town's ordinance against pornography because he wanted to avoid more negative publicity because he owned several other businesses that he did not want to suffer. In Venice, community pressure and quick legal action have made buying, selling, and even to rent pornography impossible.

Activity 24-2

Using coordinates to relate equal ideas (See 24b.)

Edit the following passage, using coordination to relate ideas of equal importance and to combine choppy sentences. More than one edited version is possible.

The workers were instructed to seal the oiled rags in cans. They forgot to do it. At night the rags caught fire. The fire spread rapidly through the storage area. A smoke detector went off. No one noticed. The alarm was relayed to the fire station. Fire fighters raced to the warehouse. Flames already were darting through the windows. Smoke poured through the ceiling. Glass cracked in the heat. It shattered. The fire commander turned in a second alarm. Another company sped toward the scene.

Activity 24-3

Avoiding ineffective coordination (See 24c.)

Edit the following passage to eliminate ineffective coordination. More than one edited version is possible.

At the start of *The Bridge Across Forever*, the narrator is a stunt pilot performing in small towns of the American Midwest, and the narrator and the author seem to have much in common. The author writes about flying, and the narrator takes people for rides in his plane, but he is bored with the routine, but he is convinced that he will find the perfect woman at one one of these shows, so he keeps going. Disillusioned at last, he gives up flying to pursue his quest, and he encounters many women, but none of them is the soul mate he is seeking.

Activity 24-4

Using subordination to distinguish main ideas (See 24d.)

Edit the following sentences, using subordination to emphasize the main idea indicated within the parentheses. You may use either subordinating conjunctions or relative clauses. More than one edited version is possible. For help, see box on page 162 of *CWR*.

1. The Sundance Kid's girlfriend was actually a prostitute in Fanny Porter's Sporting House. Hollywood portrayed the Sundance Kid's girlfriend as a schoolteacher. (Emphasize how Hollywood portrayed her.)

2. Every day thousands of Americans eat Kentucky Fried Chicken. They like their chicken "finger lickin' good." (Emphasize that thousands eat Kentucky Fried Chicken.)

3. I felt completely numb when I got my first college English paper back. The teacher had written on the bottom, "How did you get this far without getting voted off the island?" (Emphasize how you felt.)

4. The Autobahn was built by Hitler to transport tanks and troops to Germany's borders in World War II. The Autobahn is still one of the world's finest highway systems. (Emphasize who built the Autobahn.)

5. Kwanzaa has taken root as an Afro-American alternative to Christmas. Kwanzaa originated as an African harvest festival. (Emphasize that Kwanzaa has taken root.)

6. Walden Pond is now the site of many tourist stands. Walden Pond was once praised by Thoreau for its natural beauty. (Emphasize that Walden Pond was once praised by Thoreau.)

7. Men deny it. Women will soon be able to compete with them in most sporting events. (Emphasize that men deny it.)

8. Russ continues driving like a crazy man. He will lose his license soon. (Emphasize that Russ will lose his license.)

9. George Clooney starred for several years on the television show ER. George Clooney became a major box office draw for Hollywood. (Emphasize that Clooney became a box office draw.)

Activity 24-5

Avoiding ineffective subordination (See 24e.)

Edit the following passage to eliminate ineffective subordination. More than one edited version is possible.

Almost Famous is Cameron Crowe's most autobiographical film to date, although his life resembles that of the films' main character, William Miller. Even though Crowe, like William, worked as a writer for *Rolling Stone* magazine in his teens, the film's narrative of William seems to mirror Crowe's own experiences. Further proof of the film's autobiographical nature lies in Crowe's explicit description of it as a "love letter to rock-n-roll." Although his other films, which include *Jerry Maguire, Singles*, and *Say Anything*, rely heavily on rock music, none contain Crowe's obvious gratitude to the music, which has greatly influenced Crowe's filmmaking career.

Activity 24-6

Creating parallel structures (See 24f.)

Using parallelism for emphasis (See 24g.)

Strengthen sentence structures in the following paragraph by using parallelism and elliptical structures. More than one edited version is possible.

The second hit single, "Why Didn't You Call Me," from Macy Gray's On How Life Is blends a heavy loping bass line and soulful background singers. It has perfectly placed piano chops with the smoky uniqueness of Gray's voice. Such a blend seems so familiar that upon first hearing the song, one wonders what era from which the song comes. Gray's sound could place the listener in an after-hours club in the late sixties. It could also place the listener in an urban hiphop street scene.

Activity 24-7

Making parallel structures complete (See 24f–g.)

Edit the following paragraph to correct faulty parallelism. More than one edited version is possible.

First it rained, then hail was falling, and finally snow came down. As the temperature dropped, we moved our bedrolls closer to the fire, hung blankets over the windows, and more logs were added to the blaze. Nothing seemed to help. The thin walls seemed to invite the cold in. The wind whistled through cracks. The windows rattled in the wind. Snow drifted under the door.

Activity 24-8

Strengthening sentence structure (See 24a-f.)

Edit the following passage to strengthen sentence structure, using coordination, subordination, and parallel structures as you think appropriate. Many edited versions are possible.

Whether Hunter S. Thompson's world is reality or imagined, it makes for enjoyable reading. His humor arises from situations that are so frantic or such exaggerations as to be ludicrous. The writing moves from subject to subject, and it mimics the pattern of a drunken or drugged mind. His sentences ramble. His thoughts tumble. His subjects shift like colors in a hallucination. He somehow maintains a sense of reality. Each description and phrase somehow contain a sharp shard of observation. The reader gets the feeling that his scenes could have happened. Many of them are completely farfetched. He stretches our willingness to believe to the limit. This is the key to Thompson's style.

Activity 24-9

Sentence emphasis and variety (See 24a.)

Edit the following paragraph to provide emphasis and variety throughout. Be sure that sentences vary in length and type and that not all sentences begin with the subject. You may want to make deliberate use of repetition and elliptical construction and change a sentence or two to questions or exclamations. More than one edited version is possible.

I have started to observe students' body language in class only recently. Students in a group discussion, for example, reveal their moods and their reactions to others through various body movements. Students who feel that their opinions are being attacked will often cross their arms or legs. They may turn their bodies slightly from the rest of the group. This helps them feel set apart and protected. Students who are expressing an opinion they are uncertain about will often lightly touch their upper lips or their noses. This is a way of unconsciously hiding their mouths. Students who are bored or having trouble concentrating on the discussion often sit back and rest one hand on their foreheads. Students who are interested and following the discussion closely often lean forward and place one hand under their chins. Eager students are likely to fidget, shy students are likely to keep very still, and unprepared students are likely to tap their hands or feet in a rhythm. I am not sure about my own body language in these situations because I am always too busy observing everybody else. Body language, in fact, is often more interesting to me than the subject of the discussion.

Activity 24-10

Sentence emphasis and variety (See 24a.)

Edit the following passage, varying the length of the sentences to improve emphasis and variety. More than one edited version is possible.

When I heard the mail drop through the slot in the door, my heart leapt. After I practically flew downstairs, I pounced on the mail that lay scattered on the floor. There, finally, was a letter for me from Iowa State University. "Today's the day," I said to myself, "the day that will seal my fate." At last I would have the answer to the all-important question of whether I had been accepted at the school of my choice. I wondered where I would spend the next four years. I wondered if I would be in Ames, Iowa, or home in Deerfield, Illinois. After I took a deep breath and counted to three, I ripped open the envelope.

Activity 24-11

Varying sentence types (See 24a.)

Edit the following passage, varying the types of sentences to improve emphasis and variety. More than one edited version is possible.

Alcohol and alcohol abuse have been a part of our society for many centuries. Alcoholism has long been regarded as a major health problem. It is now the third greatest killer in the United States. Many individuals and organizations view alcoholism as an illness. The minds and bodies of alcoholics are ill. They are unable to control their drinking. They consequently eventually harm not only themselves but also others. Much is being done in this country to help alcoholics. Probably the best-known source is Alcoholics Anonymous. Many individual states are also starting to build centers to help alcoholics. These centers provide support and therapy. They aim to help alcoholics realize that drinking is not the answer to their problems. It is an admirable goal.

Activity 24-12

Varying sentence openings

To improve the emphasis and variety of the following passage, edit it by beginning some of the sentences with an element other than the subject. More than one edited version is possible.

The College Recruiting Network is a good resource for students and one of the best ways to get a job. The network, provided by campus career development centers, is available across the United States. Forty percent of all students make use of the service, according to studies published last year. Seniors find the network helpful most often, particularly when they don't know what they want to do when they graduate. The network was developed and implemented especially with these students in mind. Students have the opportunity to get involved in the interviewing process early on thanks to the network. Many are,

consequently, able to find a job even before they graduate.

Activity 24-13

Creating effective yet varied sentences

Edit the following sentences to create different constructions wherever you think they could be effective. Try to edit the sentences in more than one way using varied lengths, types, or openings. Choose and mark the best one you've devised for each.

1. In our family, I am the bossy one, Tom is the quiet one, and Cheryl is the friendly one.
2. Whenever we visited our grandparents' farm, we had to weed and prune in the garden until the marigolds were immaculate, the beans were beautiful, and the pea plants were pristine.
3. Our conversation would be on the virtue of hard work; our thoughts would be on the pleasures of a lazy afternoon.
4. Cheryl and I could usually convince Tom that she was too weak for this sort of work and I was too old.
5. By supper time, Tom's eyes were bleary, and his arms were exhausted, but he was happy to have finally finished.

Activity 24-14

Varying sentence openings

Edit the following passage to provide emphasis and variety throughout. Be sure that sentences vary in length and type and that not all sentences begin with the subject. Try to make use of deliberate repetition and elliptical construction. More than one edited version is possible.

Sunday dinner at Grandma's house was about as appealing as a day without recess to me, an energetic nine-year-old. It meant leaving the kids at the playing field at the bottom of the eighth inning. I had to take a bath in the middle of the day and wash behind my ears. The worst thing was that I had to put on my best clothes and try to keep them clean. For me to keep my clothes clean seemed beyond the realm of possibility in those days. My parents would look absolutely delighted as I emerged from the bath every week. I looked, frankly, nothing like myself. My father would exclaim, "She's as clean as a hound's tooth!" Yet I would arrive at Grandma's week after week looking like Raggedy Ann, despite my best efforts. My shirt would inevitably be stained, my stockings would inevitably be split, my shoes would inevitably be scuffed. My mother would look at me in disbelief as I climbed out of the car. She was amazed, no doubt that such a metamorphosis could have occurred in a twenty-minute car ride. My disheveled appearance, to be honest, never seemed to bother Grandma. She always exclaimed, "Don't you look nice!" I don't know to this day whether she was losing her eyesight or just being kind.

Concise Sentences

Activity 25-1

Editing ineffective sentences (See 25a-i.)

Edit the following passage to make it more direct and concise by deleting or simplifying wordy constructions, eliminating redundancy, simplifying grammatical constructions, and replacing pretentious or overblown language. More than one edited version is possible.

According to the administration's survey of applicants for parking stickers, one-half, or fifty percent, of the students who were questioned do not believe that parking is a problem on campus. This number is somewhat misleading, however, due to the fact that the majority of the students who answered this way are full-time residents who live on campus. It is not very likely that most residents move their vehicles on a daily basis, and when they do, they most often do so in the evening hours when spaces are maximized and easier to access. On the other hand, commuting students are compelled to do battle every single, solitary day in the never-ending war for a parking space, and they do so in the busy daytime hours between 8:00 A.M. in the morning and 12:00 noon when there are the greatest number of cars that are entering onto the campus. There is absolutely no question that these students without a doubt have the opinion that parking on campus is a problem of crucial importance, as is so clearly evidenced by the administration's survey. In point of fact, more than ninety percent of those who gave the response that parking is a problem are commuters.

Activity 25-2

Eliminating vague generalities (See 25a.)

Removing idle words (See 25b.)

Eliminating automatic and wordy phrases, useless modifiers and redundancies (25c-f.)

Edit the following passage to make it more direct and concise, eliminating vague generalities, idle words, and redundancies and simplifying grammatical constructions. More than one edited version is possible.

Many factors had an impact on the development of modern electric blues. One of the very most important of these was the migration of black country bluesmen from the Delta to Chicago. They left their farms due to the fact that they could make more money in the city. In most instances, these musicians carried only their acoustic guitars and the hope of a better life. Undoubtedly, the most famous of these musicians was Muddy Waters. He is generally credited as being the one who applied electricity to the country blues sound. Rather than playing solo on an acoustic guitar, Waters formed a band consisting of bass, drums, piano, harmonica and guitar and amplified the sound. Another Delta bluesman who had followed Waters' path to Chicago from the Delta was Howlin' Wolf. Wolf soon rivaled Waters as the best bluesman in The Windy City, and the onstage competitions between their bands were legendary. It is without a doubt that country blues musicians like Waters, Wolf, and scores of others created and defined what we now call modern electric blues. Their migration from the country to the city clearly had a more far-reaching effect than they could have forseen. White blues guitarists such as Eric Clapton, Stevie Ray Vaughan, and Jonny Lang owe a very big debt to these men.

Activity 25-3

Avoiding pretentious language (See 25h.)

Minimizing euphemism and misdirection (See 25i.)

Edit the following passage to make it more direct and concise, eliminating pretentious language, euphemism, or misdirection. More than one edited version is possible.

The photography exhibit scheduled to appear at the Mainfield Gallery has been postponed because of protests by a local community organization, which has voiced a concern about the photographic depiction of minors au naturel. This is a minority view, however. Moderates who might find fault with photographs showing acts of intimacy between consenting adults see no problem with the scheduled exhibit. And of course, those in the community who firmly espouse the sacred freedom of speech guaranteed by our forefathers would support the exhibit no matter how offensive or injurious to the moral fiber of our young people.

Activity 25-4

Creating direct and concise sentences (See 25a-i.)

Edit the following passage to make it more direct and concise. More than one edited version is possible.

My great-grandfather emigrated from Poland when he was a young man. Several of his cousins already lived in small Pennsylvania mining towns. When my great-grandfather arrived in America, he joined his cousins and began working in the mines. There were several things he found discouraging. The dirty work, which was also dangerous, was far different from the life of agricultural splendor he had expected to lead, but he refused to let these types of circumstances ruin his happiness. It eventually was the case that he brought two of his brothers over to this country, and together the three of them saved money that was sufficient to buy a good-sized farm. By the age of thirty-four, my great-grandfather had once again started a new life: he moved into his farmhouse, married a local woman, and began raising a family that would eventually be blessed by the arrival of fourteen bundles of joy.

Strong Verbs

Activity 26-1

Choosing strong verbs (See 26a–b.)

Edit the following paragraph by using strong verbs. Make any small changes in wording that are needed for smooth reading. More than one edited version is possible.

Bilingual education is becoming more of a hot topic of debate every year. Some educators make the argument that young children have a need for linguistic continuity between their homes and their classrooms. There is, in fact, a good deal of evidence that does support this view. These educators are strong advocates of programs that use a child's primary language for most classroom instruction while having him or her learn English as a second language. Over the years, the child is speaking English for more and more of the classroom day, until finally he or she is able to join a mainstream classroom.

Activity 26-2

Selecting active or passive voice (See 26d.)

Edit the following paragraph by using active voice wherever it is effective. Make any small changes in wording that are necessary for smooth reading. More than one edited version is possible.

Some college students might think that the amount of writing required of them will decrease upon entering the workplace, but they would be incorrect. According to a recent nationwide survey, employees, who had graduated within the last ten years, claim that writing comprises over sixty percent of the work they do. But is the process the same in both worlds? For junior marketing analyst and recent college graduate Pete Andreone the process is quite similar. When he is given an assignment, he starts drafting an outline. Usually after the outline is completed, research must be done. Many books and papers
are read, as well as articles from various sources. He also gathers information from various co-workers about the current marketing strategies and status of the client's project. Then writing and revising the written report ensues.

Specific Nouns and Modifiers

Activity 27-1

Using nouns effectively (See 27 a b.)

Edit the following paragraph to create more vital sentences. Substitute specific, concrete nouns and modifiers for more general ones, and replace weak or static verbs with more descriptive ones. Change passive voice verbs to the active voice where appropriate. Supply creative details wherever necessary. More than one edited version is possible.

The party was going on when I got there. Loud music was coming from the big speakers, and lots of people were on the dance floor. They looked hot and seemed unaware of their surroundings as they moved wildly to the music. As I looked around for my two friends who had got me to come, I made the observation that the walls were covered with four different colors of spirals, which made the room seem to go around. I felt a little dizzy and wanted to sit down. I tried to locate a chair, but they all seemed to be taken. Suddenly, a strange-looking person in a weird outfit came up to me. He or she—couldn't tell if it was a man or woman—said something I couldn't hear and then laughed and was gone. My stomach began to feel funny, my head was hurting, and I was nervous. "There's nothing to worry about," I told myself. "Try to have a good time."I moved through the crowd, looking for a familiar face. A drink was given to me by someone I didn't know, and it spilled all over me. I decided that it was time to go home.

Activity 27-2

Using concrete, specific nouns and modifiers (See 27a-b.)

Edit the following paragraph by using concrete, specific nouns and modifiers. You may invent and add whatever details you think are necessary. More than one edited version is possible.

Our new student union is really good. Not only does it have several dining options, but it also creates an overall pleasant dining experience. Last year, students had to eat in a temporary, makeshift cafeteria that offered little food selection or quality. The atmosphere was as unappealing as the food. Now we eat in a beautiful new setting and can choose from a variety of foods. Depending on schedule and your appetite, our revamped food services allows students to order ala cart, cafeteria style, or to go.

Activity 27-3

Adding details to make sentences more vital (See 27a-b.)

Edit the following paragraph to create vital sentences. You may invent and add any details you think are necessary. More than one edited version is possible.

Most dog owners don't realize in advance how much time, money, and energy must be spent on a puppy. First, there is housebreaking the puppy and teaching it basic puppy obedience skills: how to accompany its owner while on a leash, how to respond to its name, how to stay near its owner. There are also other things—fetching, standing, and so on. And even when owners have the time for training they probably don't have the necessary expertise. This means enrollment in expensive obedience school classes is required. Puppies have other expenses as well. Veterinarian visits, food and bedding, leashes and playthings, and grooming—a must for any well-bred dog—are all costly. And at least one nice rug or one pair of shoes must be replaced because a bad dog has chewed through them. Still, as any devoted dog owner will tell you, the expense is justified by the rewards: there's nothing like coming home from a hard day and being greeted by someone who loves you unconditionally and absolutely.

The Right Word

Activity 28-1

Improving word choice (See 28a-h.)

Edit the following passage to improve word choice. Look for problems with denotation and connotation, easily confused words, standard use of prepositions, slang, and jargon. Use a dictionary and a thesaurus, if you wish, to help you find the best word in each case. More than one edited version is possible.

The program provisions troubled adolescents with mentors who act both as roll models and as councilors. These volunteers, most of whom have experienced tempestuous childhoods themselves, can really get into the problems of teens, helping them improve self-esteem and actualize their true potentialities. During biweekly one-on-one meetings, mentors set down with program participants to help with homework, chat about any problems they may be experiencing home- or school-wise, and share impertinent life experiences. Mentors may also take participants to outings on sporting events, cultural institutes, and business settings. In addition, mentors and participants meet twice a month for group sessions under the direction of a program administrator. They discuss goals and stumble blocks, participate in consciousness-raising exercises, and strategize ways to control anger and channel positive energy. The affect has been positive on all involved.

Activity 28-2

Using the dictionary and thesaurus (See 28a.)

For each of the words below, think of as many synonyms and near synonyms as you can. Try to guess which words on your list came from Old English, which from French, which from Latin or Greek, and which from other languages. Use a dictionary to confirm your guesses. You may want to compare your word list with your classmates'.

boat

mellow

furious

fire

stranger

swig

Activity 28-3

Using the dictionary and thesaurus (See 28a.)

Use a dictionary and a thesaurus to look up any words that seem unfamiliar or that might be misused in the following passage. Edit the passage by substituting more familiar words and correcting any misuses while preserving the intended meaning.

The role of Emma Woodhouse in Jane Austen's novel *Emma* often receives censure for her supercilious behavior. Many readers consider her attitude toward her neighbors to be unconscionable: she avoids calling on them whenever possible and suffers their visits with scarcely concealed ennui. And it's certainly true that Emma regards all social functions as opportunities to display her better charms and talents. Yet Emma may be understood as Austen's portrayal of an exceptional individual constrained by a mediocre society.

Activity 28-4

Expanding your vocabulary (See 28b.)

Using context and your knowledge of prefixes, suffixes, and roots, guess the meaning of italicized words in the following sentences. Then check the accuracy of your guesses by looking up the words in a dictionary.

1. Eunice acted as though she were a *conscript* when forced to play the role of Madame Bouvard in our production.
2. She would have preferred contributing in some *nondramatic* capacity.
3. Although occasionally *immodest*, Madame Bouvard is still essentially a moral woman.
4. Because of the proximity of the furniture and the sets onstage, waltzing around requires a certain amount of *surefootedness*.
5. The script was the result of a collaborative writing project, so the real achievement lay in the *contexture*.

Activity 28-5

Considering connotations (See 28c.)

Complete the following passage, choosing one of the two words in each set of parentheses. Be sure the words you choose have the connotations you want. More than one version is possible for some sentences.

As a girl, my grandmother worked in a textile mill. Recently she (revealed to/told) me what it was like for her. Every morning she had to feed her (younger/youthful) brother and sister breakfast and then take them to the house of Cousin Sophia, who looked after them. My grandmother was at the (gates/portal) of the factory by 5:25 A.M. If an employee was late, she would (forfeit/lose) half a day's pay. The work was (drab/tedious) and exhausting. My grandmother had to (patrol/watch) and tend the same machine for hours on end, with nothing to (distract/entertain) her but the whirring and clanking of the engines. Her lunch hour was just fifteen minutes long, and she often (toiled/worked) sixteen hours a day.

Activity 28-6

Using standard idioms (See 28d & e.)

Edit the following paragraph to make sure that words and expressions are used according to convention. More than one edited version is possible.

Just a few short years ago, computers were rare as chickens' teeth on college campuses. Students had to type their papers or write them with hand, just as they had for generations. Today, however; most of us either own a word processor or have access to one owned by our schools. This has had an enormous affect both on the process we use to create papers and on the papers themselves. Some students still think they can just sit down in front of a computer the night before a paper is due, flip a switch, and crank out a paper with no real work. Most of us, however, know the truth of the computer-era saying "Garbage in, garbage out."A computer can do some of the drudgery and can make problem solving more creative, but you still have to put your face to the grindstone to write a really good paper.

Activity 28-7

Using slang, regionalisms, and colloquialisms sparingly (See 28e.)

Using jargon carefully (See 28f.)

Edit the following paragraph, making sure that slang and technical language are used only where appropriate. More than one edited version is possible.

Thirty percent of the students interviewed in the study said they owned personal computers and used them regularly to write papers. Many take basic precautions to safeguard their files, such as occasionally backing up on floppies. Most of these said they have learned through experience how important it is to take such steps. Seventy-five percent of those who own computers have trashed a file at one time or another, and almost everyone reported knowing at least one fellow hacker whose hard dish has crashed.

Activity 28-8

> **Using figurative language effectively (See 28g.)**
>
> **Eliminating clichés (See 28h.)**
>
> Edit the following passage to improve the use of figurative language. More than one edited version is possible.

That first day of school was hot as a firecracker. Heat seemed to pour from the asphalt in invisible waves as I trudged my way to this new, unknown prison. I knew that, coming from the city, I was going to be like a square peg in a round hole at this hick town high school. I wanted to run away, to join the merchant marines, anything to escape the nine months of agony that I knew was ahead of me. Why had my parents insisted on moving to the middle of nowhere in the summer before my senior year? Did they want their only son to kick the bucket before his eighteenth birthday? By the time I reached Culpepper High, I was soaked with perspiration and as unhappy as a person could possibly be.

Activity 28-9

> **Using figurative language effectively (See 28g.)**
>
> **Eliminating clichés (See 28h.)**
>
> Edit the following paragraph to improve the use of figurative language. More than one edited version is possible.

The tradition of giving up one's seat on a bus or train to elderly and disabled people has passed away. I ride the subway to and from school every day, along with lots of other people going to work or school. Everyone on the train is dog-tired, especially in the evening on the way home, and wants to sit down. Unfortunately, there just aren't enough seats for everyone. I have seen young, healthy people hurry in front of slower people, often elderly or disabled, to grab the last remaining seat. In this day and age, no one expects men to automatically give up their seats to women, but as a result, no one gives up a seat for anybody.

Activity 28-10

> **Using figurative language effectively (See 28g.)**
>
> **Eliminating clichés (See 28h.)**
>
> Edit the following paragraph to improve the use of figurative language. More than one edited version is possible.

Many people object to the television cartoon The Simpsons because they say it is over the top, but millions of children watch it with bated breath every week. Critics say shows like this are causing the American family to disintegrate and are teaching children that it is okay not to hit the books. They think that young people want to be like Bart Simpson, who is as proud as a peacock of being a bad student, and that the show is a stumbling block for students who want to be above par. I think it's crystal clear that children can tell the difference between televison and reality. When they laugh at Bart talking back to his parents, they are just letting off steam because adults are always laying down the law.

Activity 28-11

Using words effectively (See 28a-h.)

Edit the following passage, making sure that each word is the most effective. More than one edited version is possible.

Tired of getting endless heaps of mail-order catalogues in your mailbox? Don't turn on your computer for any release. If the average mail-order junkie attains ten garb catalogs, nine catalogs for housewares and garden equipment, five catalogs for a favorite hobby, and six gift catalogs each month, then that same junkie receives at least twice that many each time she gets into the Internet to look at the Web. With the hawking of mailing lists and computer programs that create buyer profiles, Internet advertising makes the mail-order catalogue business look ancient. There are a truckload of advertising options open to online advertisers that aren't available to mail-order advertisers. Some of these options include advertising through banner ads, "What's related?" buttons on search engines, and quasi-illegal spamming that occurs when you fill on an online form. These shotgun attacks of online advertising are just latest mode of junk mail.

Unbiased Language

Activity 29-1

Eliminating language that suggests any racial, ethnic, gender, or age bias (See 29a-c.)

Edit the following passage to eliminate language that suggests any racial, ethnic, gender, or age bias. More than one edited version is possible.

Most people think that policemen and firemen have the most stressful of urban jobs, but statistics show that cabdrivers suffer more on-the-job stress than either of these two groups (Seligman 192). A cabdriver puts himself at risk every hour he is on the streets, according to most of the drivers I interviewed.

Joe D'Amico is a typical Italian-American: friendly, boisterous, ready to talk your ear off no matter what the question. He's been driving a cab for five years and has been robbed three times, twice at gunpoint by drug dealer types, once at knifepoint by a well-dressed white man. "It's a jungle out there,"D'Amico says. "Fighting traffic is bad enough, but wondering every time you pick up a passenger who's going to be sitting two feet behind you is worse."

Marla Crews, an attractive mother of three who has been driving a cab for two years, agrees, "I wouldn't be doing this if the money weren't good," says Ms. Crews. "I already have an ulcer from the day-to-day stress just in the short time I've been driving."

Senior citizen Jacob Matthews, a black man who is still capable and satisfied with the job after driving a cab for almost forty years, was the only dissenter: "When you drive a cab, you have to go with the flow. I enjoy my work because I don't let it get to me. And it's better than sitting on some assembly line."

Activity 29-2

Replacing stereotypes with specifics (See 29a.)

Using labels carefully (See 29b.)

Identify stereotypes in the following passages and describe the ways in which they may be thoughtless or offensive. If any useful information is conveyed by a particular passage, edit it to communicate the information in a way that is not offensive.

1. Don't expect a nice quiet meal at this restaurant. It's labeled "kid friendly."

2. In the novel, the woman, the typical hot-blooded Italian, feels romantically repressed by her husband, a common farmer from Nebraska.

3. Without question, the undergraduates from Ivy League schools will defeat those from large public universities in next week's Jeopardy match.

4. Being Japanese, Sam ought to score extremely high on the math portion of the SAT.

5. Children raised by single males tend to exhibit less sensitive and more aggressive tendencies than those raised by two parents.

Activity 29-3

Avoiding pronouns that may alienate readers (See 29c.)

Edit the following passage to eliminate pronouns or sexist language that may offend readers. More than one edited version is possible.

Almost everyone who enters medical school expects that he will become a family practitioner when he graduates. By the time they graduate, however, the overwhelming majority of medical students have decided to specialize. The benefits of specialization are many. Some doctors are lured by the large salaries that specialists earn. They want their wives and children to be able to live in style. Many women doctors like the fact that patients' emergencies rarely disrupt a specialist's family life. But drawbacks exist as well. The number of nonspecialists has dropped so sharply that some communities find themselves without any family practitioners. What does a parent in such a community do when her child suddenly runs a fever? Whom does she call? In response to the growing problem, the government— encouraged by congressmen from those states with the greatest shortages—has begun to offer programs to encourage medical students to pursue careers in family practice. A student is given money toward medical school if he agrees to pursue a career in family practice when he graduates. Increasing numbers of students are taking this option, and many are finding that the personal rewards more than compensate for the smaller salary.

Activity 29-4

Eliminating biased language (See 29a-c.)

Edit the following passage, eliminating any biased language that may be offensive to readers. More than one edited version is possible.

All of the old people at White Pines Residence agree that there couldn't be a better place for them to live. The modern residence has been designed to meet their every need, and in some ways it resembles a spa more than an old-age home. For one thing, the food is terrific. Every meal offers at least one exotic dish, always cooked to perfection. This isn't surprising, considering that the chef was born in Paris. In the medical area, facilities and services are first rate. A doctor is on call around the clock to provide care to all of the residents, many of whom suffer from cancer. With the handicapped in mind, doorways have been built that are wide enough for a cripple's wheelchair to pass through, and ramps are familiar sights, both inside and outside. Staff members have been carefully chosen for both their experience with old people and their personalities. They are all extremely popular with the residents. One of the best loved is a male nurse who always makes time in his busy schedule to read to the blind residents. Another nurse is a former actress; she has arranged for a local theater group to perform regularly at the residence. In addition, volunteers from the local college visit with the residents, providing them with companionship and friendship. Like so many old people, the residents at White Pines enjoy spending time with young people and telling stories about their youth. State-of-the-art facilities are not cheap, however, and White Pines is no exception; the cost of the facility may explain the high percentage of Jewish residents. To judge from the level of satisfaction among the residents, however, it is money well spent.

Proofreading

Activity 30-1

Proofreading for spelling, grammar, punctuation, and mechanics

Proofread the following passage, correcting all errors in spelling, grammar, punctuation, and mechanics. Use standard proofreading marks.

Originally panned by critic as noting more then a cheap shocker, Alfred Hitchcocks film "Psycho" is now considered a cult classic and one of the directors greatest achievements. What most people remember best about the movie is the famous shower scene, in which Janet Leigh is attacked by knive-wielding old lady. (Some film historians have argue that this scene was not acutally directed by Hitchcock but by Saul Bass his assistant director. However, their are many other effective moments: The long introduction showing Janet Leigh stealing money from the bank were she works and driving thorough the night to the Bates motel, the detective, played by Martin Balsam, climbing the stair case in the old house as he looks for Mrs. Bates, and, of course the climatic scene in the basement when Vera Miles come face to face with with the skeleton of Mrs. Bates. Alos adding alot to the suspense of the movie is the sharp, black and white photography by John L. Russell, the intnese music by Bernard Herrmann, and the truely eerie performance by Anthony Perkins' in the central role of Norman/Mrs. Bates. A critic is entitled to their opinion, but most of them were wrong about "Psycho" in 1960.

Activity 30-2

Proofreading for spelling, grammar, punctuation, and mechanics

Proofread the following passage, correcting all errors in spelling, grammar, punctuation, and mechanics. Use standard proofreading marks.

Marian Anderson, who died in 1993, was the first black opera singer to preform at the Metropoliton Opera (1955), and she became an inspiration to generations of black performers thoughout the U.S. Yet she was not able to make a name for herself in her own county until late in her life because of raical discrimmination. Althrough her grate talent was recognised early in her life (she won a voice contest in New York in 1925,) she could not get any rolls in opera, and her carrer was going nowhere. In the 1930s, Anderson decided to go to Europe to perform, and she quickly became an international singing star. When she returned to the U.S. and was invited to sing in Washington, DC, the D.A.R. (Daughters of the American Revolution) denied her acess to Constitution Hall, it's national headquarters. Eleanor Roosveit (along with several other women) resined from the D.A.R. over this disgracefull incident, and she aranged for Anderson to perform outside at the Lincoln Memorial. 75,000 people came to hear Anderson sing, and her performance in front of Lincolns statute became a powerful cymbal of the civil right's movement.

Activity 30-3

Proofreading for spelling, grammar, punctuation, and mechanics

Proofread the following passage, correcting all errors in spelling, grammar, punctuation, and mechanics. Use standard proofreading marks.

Erma Bombeck (1927–1996), columnist and author of 9 books and countless articels, use wit and sarcasm in telling her tales of housewife reppresion and thankless child rearing. Her own experence in the fields of mother hood and mariage are the largest facter contributeing to the credability of her stories. Writen primarily between 1970–1979, Bobeck's works are humourous attempts at understanding the most-pressing problems of the seventies, the two predominant ones delt with her writing are the underated house-wife and the increasing number of teenagers. Her books are all written in a similer stile: they are collections of stories based on her personal experienses and are filled with humor, vivacity, and cleverness. Having viewed Bombeck's televised commentaries and read her books and articles, she is obviously able to find humor in everything she encounters. That humor is often convayed threw sarcasm, and she can be down-right negative and pessimistic, yet Bombeck is always abel to maintain a light-hearted and very funny style.

Commas

Activity 31-1

Using commas correctly (See 31a-j.)

Edit the following passage, making sure that commas are used where required.

In the election year 2000 a trend in American politics emerged: more women assumed positions of power. And while the trend is encouraging, America still lags behind many other developed nations in this area. In 2000 thirteen women took their seats in the Senate chamber and fifty-nine women filled positions in the House. Furthermore George W. Bush became the first Republican president in U.S. history to make white males a minority in his own cabinet. Despite the optimistic increase in the House and Senate (thirteen percent and fourteen percent respectively) America still trails other nations in electing women leaders. For example in Germany, the Netherlands, and the Scandinavian countries, women hold more than twenty-five percent of seats in the lower houses of parliament. Furthermore, America has not yet placed women in the ultimate position of power the presidency like other developed countries have. The names of many past and present women leaders of other countries spring easily to mind including Gandhi Thatcher Bhutoo and Meir. And since 1997 several more have added their names to the list: Mary McAleese president of Ireland in 1997, Helen Clark prime minister of New Zealand in 1999 and Tarja Kaarina Halonen president of Finland in 2000. We as Americans are beginning to model our global neighbors in electing women to powerful political positions but it may be a while before we see a woman in the White House.

Activity 31-2

Using commas before coordinating conjunctions joining independent clauses (See 31a.)

Edit the following sentences with coordinating conjunctions joining independent clauses, using commas correctly. Circle the number of any sentence that is correct.

1. Every new business or residence along a highway needs an access road but first the highway department must approve its design and location.

2. The developer of a new housing development or commercial center must complete an application, and must submit it for the highway department's review.

3. The standards for sight distances and markings are very clearly described in the regulations so a developer can tell if a driveway is acceptable.

4. The minimum sight distances vary with the speed limit and the grade of the road and the standards for driveway construction vary with the expected volume of traffic.

5. The highway department does not have to permit a driveway that does not meet its standards or that would require modifications to the roadway.

Activity 31-3

Using commas before coordinating conjunctions joining independent clauses (See 31a.)

Edit the following sentences by using a comma and a coordinating conjunction to join two sentences into one sentence. Most sentences can be edited in more than one way.

1. DNA testing can be used as evidence to convict criminals. It can also be used to free many who have been wrongly incarcerated.

2. By mid-1999 more than sixty people had been released from prison. Many of them had already served a number of years behind bars.

3. Initially, legal experts questioned the reliability of DNA testing. Even the strongest critics soon recognized the conclusiveness of DNA evidence.

4. They could not ignore the numerous advances in DNA technology. They could not ignore the growing use of DNA testing as evidence.

5. The FBI recognized the universal application of this powerful investigative tool for our country. The FBI launched the National DNA Index System, a nationwide computer database, into which states could submit samples from known criminals and from unknown persons at crime scenes.

Activity 31-4

Using commas before coordinating conjunctions joining independent clauses (See 31a.)
Using commas after introductory elements (See 31b.)

Edit the following passage, making sure that commas are used correctly with introductory elements and with coordinating conjunctions in compound sentences.

Originally called the "Women's Liberation Movement" the women's movement as we know it was founded during the 1960s. Although the impact of the modern women's movement should not be underestimated the campaign for greater rights for women did not begin at that decade. More than a century earlier the first women's rights convention convened in the New York town of Seneca Falls and its main purpose was to address the issue of a woman's right to vote. Elizabeth Cady Stanton and Lucretia Mott were both prominent abolitionists in the 1840s and they also campaigned hard for women's rights. The nineteenth-century movement succeeded in convincing thousands of men and women that women should have the vote but women's suffrage did not become a reality until 1920, with the 19th Amendment.

38

Activity 31-5

Using commas after introductory elements (See 31b.)

Edit the following passage, using commas after introductory elements.

When she met Alfred Stieglitz Georgia O'Keeffe was studying at the Art Students League. Then twenty years old O'Keeffe visited Stieglitz's famous 291 gallery and became acquainted with the pioneering photographer. About eight years later she sent some drawings to a friend, and the friend showed them to Stieglitz. Without asking her permission he hung them in his gallery. She demanded that he take them down, but he did not. Nearly a year later he mounted a solo exhibit of her work, and their alliance was fully established.

Activity 31-6

Using commas to set off nonrestrictive modifiers and appositives (See 31c.)

Edit the following passage, using commas with nonrestrictive modifiers and appositives.

Musical genius that sometimes overused term has been applied to popular musicians for various reasons. Stevie Wonder one of the most famous blind musicians of the twentieth century has received the moniker. He demonstrates amazing proficiency and creativity in playing not only various keyboard instruments, but also the chromatic harmonica one of the most difficult wind instruments to master. Given that he is blind, his accomplishments seem to warrant such a designation. Another musician who has been honored with the term is Prince. He plays a variety of instruments guitars, keyboards, and drums and writes songs which incorporate a multitude of musical influences. His groundbreaking album Purple Rain which won the 1985 Grammy for "Album of the Year" best illustrates his immense abilities. The latest artist who has garnered the genius distinction is Beck whose real name is Beck Hansen. His eclectic blend of various musical styles, interesting lyrics, and the ability to play numerous instruments have prompted music critics use the term when referring to him. To their credit, these musicians possess abundant talent, but given the frequency with which the term is applied, one wonders what today's music critic would have called Mozart.

Activity 31-7

Using commas to set off nonrestrictive modifiers and appositives (See 31c.)

Edit the following passage, making sure that commas are used correctly with restrictive and nonrestrictive modifiers and appositives. More than one edited version is possible.

No one, who has been to the top of Mount Battie on the coast of Maine, can fail to be struck by the scenic beauty of the landscape, which is visible for miles. It is easy to appreciate the feelings, which inspired American poet, Edna St. Vincent Millay, to write her famous poem, "Renascence." At the top of the mountain near a bronze plaque that commemorates the veterans, who fought in World War I, is a plaque, explaining that Millay wrote her poem while enjoying the view from the summit. The magnificent view, which inspired her, is virtually unchanged today, and thousands of visitors go to Mount Battie every year to enjoy the same sweeping views of the mountains and the sea.

Activity 31-8

Using commas to set off nonrestrictive modifiers and appositives (See 31c.)

Edit the following sentences to make sure that commas are used correctly with modifiers and appositives. Circle the number of any sentence that is correct.

1. The workers in the pasteurization room who are all dressed alike wear white uniforms, blue hats, black boots, and belts.
2. Manager Karen Owens explained that the cows that she keeps include Holsteins, Jerseys, and Guernseys.
3. The farm's pasteurizer whose pipes carry milk back and forth and through a coil heats milk for fifteen minutes and then quickly cools it.
4. Of the two homogenizers, the machine, on the left, has pistons at the front, designed to force the milk through small valves.
5. In the last part of the system which is the packaging machine heat lamps melt wax, and the containers get shaped and sealed.

Activity 31-9

Using commas between elements in a series and between coordinate adjectives (See 31e.)

Edit the following sentences, using commas correctly between items in a series and between coordinate adjectives. Circle the number of any sentence that is correct.

1. Inside the airport are a comfortable lounge, three departure gates, and a restaurant.
2. The airport leases the space to a number of customers, including airlines car rental agencies food concessions and gift shops.

3. The airport's representative explained that the airport is run like larger airports that it leases out its buildings and that it takes a percentage of the profits made by the independent businesses.

4. The majority of air travel at the airport is between Boston Newark and Chicago, although travel is by no means limited to these three, major cities.

5. Over the next ten years, the airport hopes to replace the few, remaining pre-1950s buildings with large modern facilities.

Activity 31-10

Using commas to set off parenthetical elements (See 31d.)

Edit the following sentences, using commas correctly with parenthetical expressions. Circle the number of any sentence that is correct.

1. "Is today in fact the day the papers are due?" I have heard that question more often than I choose to remember let me tell you.

2. Since weekly papers are due every Monday, it should come as no surprise although it often does when Monday rolls around with such relentless regularity.

3. Just this morning, for example, some students asked me whether I might allow them to turn in Monday's paper on Tuesday.

4. "Certainly," I replied. I added however that today's essay submitted tomorrow should be worth at least as much as yesterday's newspaper delivered today.

5. "However, there is you should know one important difference between a newspaper company and me. A newspaper company on the one hand gives credit for a paper that is one day late, while I on the other hand do not."

Activity 31-11

Using commas to set off elements of contrast, tag sentences, and words of direct address (See 31g.)

Edit the following sentences, using commas correctly to set off elements of contrast, tag questions, and words of direct address.

Circle the number of any sentence that is correct.

1. Most people over seventy-five own their homes my friends not because they have a lot of money but because they purchased them years ago, when housing prices were low.

2. Often elderly people who want to be independent have to live in conditions they consider less than ideal don't they?

3. The children of the elderly, not the elderly themselves, tend to worry about illness and accidents.

4. The growing numbers of people over age eighty-five are in better not worse condition than their predecessors.

5. Given that they are in better condition, many are able if not eager to live alone.

Activity 31-12

Using commas with quotations (See 31h.)

Edit the following sentences, using commas correctly with quotations.

1. "I don't know"Danielle replied "but I think that Terry has a good chance."

2. "Did Dolores say anything about the current," Danielle inquired?"Where is it strongest?"

3. Isabella replied "The current is strongest in the deepest part of the channel, but the seaweed in the shallow parts can really slow the boat down."

4. As the gun went off, Isabella muttered "If we lose this race, then all the time and effort that we spent will be for nothing!"

Activity 31-13

Using commas with numbers, dates, names, and places (See 31i.)

Edit the following sentences, using commas correctly with numbers, dates, names, and addresses.

1. I started my job in February, 2000, and the last day I worked was January 15 2001.

2. During that time, I answered 3456 calls and sold merchandise worth more than $200000.

3. The worst customers are the ones with names like Jane Jones Ph.D. or John Johnson, III, who insist on having their titles appear on all their mail.

4. You may write to my former employer at this address: National Mail-Order Products, 19123 Fifth Avenue New York New York 10001.

5. With $1500 in my saving account, I do not need to worry about getting another job until March 2003.

Activity 31-14

Using commas to prevent misreading (See 31j.)

Edit the following sentences, inserting commas wherever necessary to prevent misreading.

1. What the defendant's alibi is simply incredible.

2. Before the defendant was involved in similar crimes.

3. They are to listen to the prosecutor and defense lawyer and judge the defendant as they deem fit.

4. The verdict came in record time.

5. In keeping with what is permitted by the law firm punishment is expected.

Activity 31-15

Avoiding the misuse of commas

Edit the following passage by deleting any unnecessary commas. For help, see box on pp. 202-204 of *CWR*.

All of the students who live in the co-op on campus, work together, to keep the place clean. It usually takes about half an hour to clean the dorm, and each person cleans twice a month. The job of the "whip" is, to make sure the cleaning is done. If the job has not been done, when the whip checks it, the student, who is responsible, is given a demerit point. Students must accumulate fewer than three demerit points, or be forced to move out of the co-op. If the whip says that, a job has been done poorly, the student has to do it again. Cleaning up after others, is not a lot of fun, but I have to admit that, the co-op is the cleanest dorm on campus.

Activity 31-16

Avoiding the misuse of commas

Edit the following sentences, deleting any unnecessary commas. Circle the number of any sentence that is correct. For help, see box on pp. 202-204 of *CWR*.

1. What made this year special, was that, I was entering college.

2. I had to confess that, the thought of being in a school with thousands of students, made me nervous.

3. A bit unsure of what to expect, but also excited, I got out of bed.

4. What seemed to fear most, was that I would make embarrassing mistakes, and humiliate myself in front of thousands of strangers.

5. Not surprisingly a number of things did go wrong, but I told myself that life could only get better.

Activity 31-17

Using commas correctly

Edit the following passage, using commas correctly.

Recently descendants of the Vikings achieved what their ancestors had failed to do a millennium earlier—conquer the eastern Canadian province of Newfoundland. Instead of using swords spears, and shields the latter-day Norsemen used songs, sagas and a fleet of graceful replica ships to win over the people of this rocky island where Vikings led by Leif Erikkson briefly settled in about AD 1000. One replica ship Islendingur was greeted by more than 15000 people who had climbed steep rocks to witness its arrival on the grassy reaches of

L'Anse aux Meadows. After emerging from the fog storms and towering icebergs of the North Atlantic Capt. Gunnar Eggertsson an Icelander and descendant of Erikkson said "L'Anse aux Meadows was a very special place. There we saw houses that had been there since the year 1000 and we also saw the houses where people live that were like the houses we build in Iceland today."

Semicolons

Activity 32-1

Using semicolons correctly and effectively (See 32a-c)

Edit the following passage, using semicolons where they are correct and effective.

That summer the river rose higher than anyone thought possible. No one alive had ever seen anything like it, in fact, it had never been so high—not since the county started keeping records. Every morning when we woke up, we would go to the windows; hoping to make out even one ray of sunlight slanting through the clouds. But day after day after day we saw only gray—gray clouds, gray rain, gray skies. The sun was nowhere to be seen. We tuned in to the radio constantly. It was our only link with the outside world. The station broadcast around the clock, keeping us up-to-date on every aspect of the flood; the latest relief efforts, where volunteers were needed next, and, of course, the latest weather forecast. We river people are stubborn, I guess. For a long time, nobody was willing to leave. We had all seen heavy rains before, and we had always come out all right. So we stayed on; hoping that today might bring the change we were looking for. By the ninth day, the town's fresh water supply ran out. Most people finally gave up and evacuated. But some people still refused to go; even though staying now meant they risked losing more than their homes. They had lived there all their lives, life anywhere else was simply unimaginable. It took about a month; but the river did eventually subside. How we got rid of the mud is another story.

Activity 32-2

Using semicolons between independent clauses (See 32a.)

Edit the following sentences, using semicolons as necessary to join independent clauses.

1. Some famous athletes begin their rise to stardom almost from the day they are born, but it takes more than athletic talent to insure their fame, the media plays a major role doing that.

2. For example, a five-year old Andre Agassi appeared on The Tonight Show, demonstrating an already commanding forehand stroke, as an adult, he went on to a number one ranking on the pro tennis circuit, consistently appearing on television both as an athlete and as an adman for numerous products.

3. But it is golfer Tiger Woods who provides the most dramatic example of an early rise to stardom that the media has promoted, even earlier than Agassi, he debuted his immense talent on The Mike Douglass Show at the age of two.

4. Of course Woods has become arguably the most famous athlete in the world, for example, people from other countries who have never even heard of golf know his name.

5. They know his name because his sports agent develops a marketing strategy, securing appropriate endorsements, and scheduling timely public appearances, to insure consistent media coverage, ultimately, however, Woods must win tournaments.

Activity 32-3

Using semicolons between independent clauses (See 32a.)

Edit the following pairs of sentences, using a semicolon to join them. Add conjunctive adverbs, transitional expressions, or coordinating conjunctions if appropriate to express the relationships between the sentences. Some sentences can be edited in more than one way.

1. The shelter gives the homeless free food, does not impose a limit to the number of nights they can stay, and does not require guests to do any work around the place. Many of the young people treat it like one big party.
2. The shelter's intentions are only the best. The results are less than desirable.
3. The manager of the Salvation Army shelter, who is an ordained minister, runs the thrift store, oversees the soup kitchen, performs church services, and supervises fundraising efforts. He still finds time to visit with the residents every night.
4. Many homeless people tend either to go someplace warmer in the winter or to find more permanent living arrangements. Attendance at area shelters actually goes down.
5. Many people who use the East Side shelter are either working or have found a place to live within six weeks of leaving the shelter. That emergency shelter's success rate is 80 percent.

Activity 32-4

Using semicolons between independent clauses (See 32a.)

Edit the following passage, using semicolons between independent clauses wherever you think they are effective. More than one edited version is possible.

At the beginning, many people referred to it as the "growth bill," for its point was to help towns regain some control over the growing development that threatened their way of life. For the bill to succeed, participation among town residents was strongly encouraged. In fact, citizen participation was key. Some of the citizens, who had a bad relationship with local officials, were skeptical. Others were willing to give it a try. In the case of one supporter, repeated examples of poor planning and improper zoning eventually got to him, and, finally, he just had to get involved.

Activity 32-5

Using semicolons in a series containing commas (See 32c.)

Edit the following sentences, using semicolons as necessary in complex series.

1. Several different craft can be seen on the Charles Rivers, including sculls rowed by students from the universities in the area, canoes, rowboats, which can be rented for a small fee, and motorboats.

2. To get to know a new place quickly, obtain a detailed map of the area you plan to visit, walk to as many places as possible, always wearing shoes with good soles, and talk to the residents, provided they look friendly.

3. If you go to Boston's Museum of Fine Arts, don't miss the Paul Revere silver, the Egyptian mummies, the Athenian vases, and the terrific collection of paintings, including works by Gauguin, Degas, Monet, van Gogh, and Whistler.

4. If you really want to fit in, ask someone where the locals eat, find out how to get there, using public transportation, of course, and get to your destination without even consulting your subway map.

5. New England has produced some of the greatest writers in America: Henry David Thoreau, who wrote, Walden, Henry Wasdworth Longfellow, whose house on Brattle Street in Cambridge is a historic landmark, and Nathaniel Hawthorne, a resident of Salem, Massachusetts, and author of The Scarlet Letter.

Activity 32-6

Avoiding misuses of semicolons

Edit the following sentences by placing any incorrectly used semicolons with the correct mark of punctuation or rewording the sentence. Some sentences can be edited in more than one way. Circle the number of any sentence that is correct. For help, see box on p. 206 of *CWR*.

1. His writing abounds with examples of the greedy nature of human beings; however, it does not convey a sense of helplessness.

2. Mowat clings to a spark of hope that it is not too late for humans to develop a respectful attitude toward our planet and the animals that inhabit it; although he regards humans as covetous.

3. A self-designated advocate for nonhuman animals, Mowat reveals the precariousness of the relationship between humans and animals; with unforgiving honesty for the most part.

4. He can be delightfully witty when describing a positive and healthy relationship but also merciless in his condemnation; especially when it is destructive and exploitative, as it is more often than not.

5. After describing the harsh conditions in the village of Burgeo in the north of Newfoundland, he reveals the lure of the place; abundant fish, seals, dolphins, and whales.

Activity 32-7

Editing ineffective semicolons

Edit the following passage so that it includes only those semicolons that are effective.

Let there be no doubt that George Will is the quintessential conservative, and a widely read one at that; his message has a way of permeating the nation's political ear. He is perhaps the most widely syndicated columnist of the last decade; at least four hundred newspapers carry his column. His thoughts are expressed regularly in magazines, and his books have been reviewed by countless journals; however, no reviewer seems to agree with all of Will's ideas. Will seems to think that he knows what America needs to hear; America, for its part, seems to be listening.

Activity 32-8

Using semicolons effectively

Edit the following passage, using semicolons correctly. More than one edited version is possible.

What I like best about Spalding Gray's writing is that it is so personal. He tells the reader not only what happened, but also how he felt. Although some of the experiences he writes about are somewhat out of the ordinary, he always manages to find something everyone can relate to. Gray is not just a writer, though. He's also a monologist and an actor. He did not write down his first ten monologues, the first of which was an exercise in his acting class. Instead, he simply told them over and over. In fact, when Gray first started writing down his stories; he found it very difficult. He felt as if he had lost his personal voice and rhythm. He decided in the end to rework the transcripts of his monologues from his performances and put them into writing. Luckily, he was successful. He managed to preserve his unique and personal quality, and now, whether his story is told in person or on the page; it is absolutely riveting.

Colons

Activity 33-1

Using colons correctly (See 33a-b.)

Edit the following passage, making sure that colons are used correctly to introduce examples, explanations, lists, and quotations and to separate certain elements.

After my last semester of college, four of my friends and I rented a house by the ocean for one week. We had one goal in mind to be together one last time before we would go our separate ways. Our vacation turned out to be idyllic. During the day, we: went to the beach, read dive-store novels that we found in the basement, and worked on a 1,500-piece jigsaw puzzle, which had a biblical theme; the Last Supper. Around 7.00 we would have our dinner and then spend the evening: talking, watching a movie, or playing a game. We usually played one of three games: Scrabble, charades, or one that my friends and I invented, called: "Literary Quotations." The game is played as follows, one person suggests a subject, and each player tries to come up with a quotation from literature on that subject. For example: one night Emma proposed "sleep" as a theme, and Pamela promptly spoke these lines from Homer's Odyssey, "There is a time for words and there is also a time for sleeping." Bob added these words from Cervantes's Don Quixote, "Blessings light upon him that first invented this same sleep!" LeeAnn spoke up, "As Hamlet said: 'To sleep—perchance to dream: ay there's the rub.'" The game sounds difficult, but I surprised myself with how many times I was able to remember fitting quotes. I guess my four years as an English major were worth it after all!

Activity 33-2

Using colons as marks of introduction (See 33a.)

Using colons as marks of separation (See 33b.)

Edit the following sentences, using colons correctly. Circle the number of any sentence that is correct.

1. The tone of my father's voice could mean only one thing, I was in trouble.

2. Taking off on a cross-country trip all alone, the young boy thought of three things: freedom, freedom, freedom.

3. Perhaps the most famous opening lines from a presidential speech come from Lincoln's Gettysburg Address, "Four score and seven years ago, . . ."

4. The sight of my first whale made me think of Jonah 1.17-2.10.

5. The exact time of the shuttle launch was 12.16.42.

6. The resurgence of the scooter has led to an increase in emergency room visits: Last year, 44,000 teens saw ER doctors.

7. It seems that little league coaches these days stress just one thing: winning.

8. The film American Beauty defied expectations; it became a critical as well as popular success despite its subject matter.

9. According to family lore, my mother has set her alarm clock for 530 a.m. since she was eleven years old.

10. One more school assignment awaited me however, revising sentences that need one or more colons.

Activity 33-3

Avoiding misuses of colons

Edit the following sentences, using a colon correctly in each one. Some sentences can be edited in more than one way. Circle the number of any sentence that is correct. For help, see box on p. 209 of *CWR*.

1. For many years before war actually broke out, Britain kept demanding: that the increasingly prosperous and independent colonies pay taxes to Britain.

2. The colonists rebelled, basing their resistance on the principle: that there should be no taxation without representation in the British Parliament.

3. Two major events that occurred in the Boston area were: the Boston Tea Party and the Boston Massacre.

4. Paul Revere, immortalized in a poem by Henry Wadsworth Longfellow, rode on horseback to Lexington: to issue a warning to the Minutemen that the British were coming.

5. Important battles of the Revolutionary War include the following Massachusetts battles: Lexington, Concord, and Bunker Hill.

Activity 33-4

Using semicolons correctly (See 33a-b)
Edit the following passage, using colons correctly and deleting colons that are used incorrectly. More than one edited version is possible.

Last summer, while I was painting a house adjacent to a retirement home, I got a chance to spend time with some of the residents. Ten to twenty older men would congregate in what they called "The Pub," a room that contained: tables comfortable chairs, a small bar, a pool table, and a television set. Each day at exactly 430 P.M. the social hour at the pub began for the staff and residents. I got to know a few of these men and learned to appreciate their special qualities, their personalities, their keen senses of humor; and their phenomenal memories. One resident liked to quote: the following lines from Yeats's "Sailing to Byzantium"—"An aged man is but a paltry thing. / A tattered coat upon a stick, unless / Soul clap its hand and sing, and louder sing / For every tatter in its mortal dress." At this point sometimes someone would applaud and say:"Encore!"These very special men had seen many days, that they still had much life in them. They seemed very wise to me: aged in the finest sense of the word.

End Punctuation

Activity 34-1

Using periods, exclamation points and question marks correctly (See 34a-c.)

Edit the following passage, making sure that periods, exclamation points, and question marks are used correctly.

Many people have asked me what it takes to be a successful triathlon competitor? Incredible physical stamina. An obsessive personality. A bit of both? I guess it does take a particular personality. Let's face it: sweating and straining for more than an hour isn't everyone's idea of a good time, is it. My last triathlon, for example, was probably the most difficult I have ever completed. It started out well enough. In fact, I couldn't believe how easy the 3/4-kilometer swim was for me. The next phase of the race was the 20-kilometer bicycle race. Was that ever hard? The Santa Fe course is challenging at the best of times, but on that day, a drizzle had begun falling at around 6:00 A.M. By the time the race began, the road surface was dangerously slick. In a race in the Southwest, I never expected—who would—to encounter such treacherous conditions for biking. Wouldn't you know that the one day it would rain in months would be the day of our race? The ride went better than I had expected, considering I had to ride more slowly than usual. And am I glad I did? Right in front of me, the Michigan woman's back wheel slid out from under her. Talk about a nerve-wracking ride. By the time I started the 5-kilometer road race at the end, I was so tense that I couldn't find a good stride. I never did make up the lost time, and, even though my finishing time was under two hours—can you believe it!—I felt terrible at the end. But I never let a bad race make me discouraged. There's always another race, isn't there.

Activity 34-2

Using periods at the ends of sentences (See 34a.)

Using periods with abbreviations (See 34a.)

Using question marks (See 34b.)

Edit the following sentences by using periods correctly.

1. Because he is so interested in the 5th century B.C., Carlos usually does well on ancient history tests.

2. He especially likes the period ca 455–430 B.C., when Athenian culture was at its height.

3. The note on the board reads: "For tomorrow's test, please read Chapter 7 (pp 100–133)."

4. Rob asks if he can borrow Carlos's notes to study for the test?

5. Rob sometimes wonders how much studying will be enough?

Activity 34-3

Using question marks (See 34b.)

Edit the following sentences by using question marks correctly.

1. I wonder how long it takes to be able to think in a different language?

2. What is the best way for me to learn to speak French. Converse with my friends. Go to the language lab. Go to France?

3. The best way to learn to speak another language is to speak it as often as possible, isn't it.

4. Some students think it's entertaining (?) when classmates make mistakes.

5. You know, don't you, that we learn by making mistakes.

Activity 34-4

Using exclamation points (See 34c.)

Edit the following sentences by using exclamation points correctly. Some sentences have more than one possible answer.

1. "Look out," he called out as the dog ran in front of me.

2. "Get out of the way! Otis!" I shouted. "I'm trying to carry the groceries."

3. "Oh! I'm sure he understood that."

4. "How many times have I told you not to let the dog out?"

5. "Don't blame me?" she exclaimed. "He's your dog; not mine."

Activity 34-5

Using end punctuation correctly (See 34a-c)

Edit the following passage by using all end punctuation correctly. More than one edited version is possible.

What a morning. I wonder if you ever had the kind of morning when everything seems to go wrong? First I overslept (!) because my alarm clock didn't go off Then I was hurrying to make my class and I tripped and fell and skinned my knee. I rushed into the classroom and saw my classmates clearing off their desks and taking out clean sheets of paper? I asked someone whether we were having a test? She whispered back, "Don't you remember. It's our Roman history test. On the collapse of the empire!" Of course. How could I have forgotten. "When was that," I whispered. "It was 133-31 B.C.," she whispered back. Then Professor Martin wanted to know why I wasn't sitting down? Was I planning to join the rest of the class today. "What else can I do now?," I muttered under my breath as I took my seat. "All right, everybody," he said. "On your mark. Get set. Go. Start writing."

Apostrophes

Activity 35-1

Using apostrophes correctly (See 35a-c.)

Edit the following passage, making sure that apostrophes are used correctly.

Imagine the flurry of excitement that must have rippled through the room at the mathematicians's meeting in Cambridge, England in the spring of 93. Until that day, no one had ever dreamt that Fermat's Last Theorem would one day be proved. No one except Princeton Universitys Andrew Wiles, that is, who's lifelong obsession had been to find the proof that had eluded Ph.D.s for more than 350 years. Finding it's proof had nagged at Wiles most of his' life, even as a child, when he first came across the theorem in a library book. Pierre de Fermat worked out his' famous theorem in 1637, jotting it down in the margin of a book. He did'nt have room, however, for the theorems proof of the books' margin. He had room only to explain, that, although he'd worked out a wonderful proof for his theorem, he did'nt have room to show it. For seven year's before he solved it, Wiles attention was directed almost exclusively toward proving the theorem, but almost no one knew what he was working on. Rumors circulated at the mathematicians's meeting when it became known that Wiles would speak on Fermat's last theorem. Little did the participants expect, however, that they're colleague had actually solved the most famous puzzle of modern mathematics.

Activity 35-2

Using apostrophes to form the possessive case of nouns and indefinite pronouns (See 35a.)

Edit the following sentences, using apostrophes correctly to form the possessive of nouns and indefinite pronouns. Circle the number of any sentence that is correct.

1. The childrens spirits lifted when they saw the snow accumulating, since they knew it was their local school boards' tendency to close for inclement weather.

2. To many peoples' surprise, schools were open.

3. The storms' gale force winds howled for hours, and their strength caused a branch of my neighbors' oak tree to snap.

4. Stranded passenger's cars could be seen dotting the turnpike, abandoned in the storms' white-out conditions.

5. For most people, it will be several day's work to extricate their cars from the snow and ice.

6. The various cities' snow removal budgets were depleted even before the blizzard's first flakes fell.

7. The day before the storm hit, grocery store's long checkout lines attested to everyones expectations that they would be snowed in for a long time.

8. The storm's devastation could be seen from New England to Florida. Without a doubt it caused the eastern state's worst damage of the century.

Activity 35-3

Using apostrophes to form certain plurals (See 35b.)

Edit the following sentences, using apostrophes where needed to form plurals and eliminate unnecessary apostrophes. Circle the number of any sentence that is correct.

1. During the 1960s, enrollments in U.S. colleges and universities increased dramatically.

2. To meet the demand of this rapid increase in students, colleges and universities hired professors who held only M.A.s.

3. While these institutions wanted to hire Ph.D.'s exclusively, they needed faculty members to teach their growing curriculum.

4. Therefore, A.B.D.s, which stands for "all but dissertation," were considered first.

5. Hundred's, perhaps thousand's, of M.A.s were hired during this time and many went on to complete their Ph.D.s.

Activity 35-4

Using apostrophes to form contractions (See 35c.)

Edit the following sentences, using apostrophes correctly to form contractions.

1. In the summer there's a boat that takes passengers from the city to Bear Mountain, where hiking enthusiasts wont be disappointed.

2. The views from the mountain's 1300-foot summit cant be surpassed; youll see wilderness stretching out before your eyes in every direction.

3. A trip to the country wouldnt be complete without a stop at Buddy's Café n Deli.

4. Hyde Park is home to FDR's country mansion, which has been preserved as it was when he died in 45.

5. You cant go wrong in the Hudson River Valley if what you like is stunning scenery, great hiking possibilities and rich history.

Activity 35-5

Avoiding misuses of the apostrophe

Edit the following sentences, being careful to distinguish plurals, contractions, and possessives. For help, see box on p. 215 of *CWR*.

1. Its perhaps surprising to learn that Dickens didn't start out as a novelist; instead, he trained as a lawyer's clerk.

2. The author, who's literary career began during the 1830's started out writing for magazines' under the pseudonym "Boz."

3. Society's evil, corruption, and crime were concerns to Dickens, and their frequently found as themes throughout his novels.

4. They're style and structure were affected by the fact that Dickens wrote his novel's for publication in monthly installments.

5. Dickens's first novel was Pickwick Papers, who's monthly installments were accompanied by plates created by a popular artist.

Activity 35-6

Using apostrophes correctly

Edit the following passage, using apostrophes correctly.

In ancient Athens, after some of the Acropolis early buildings were destroyed by the Persians during the Persian War; the Athenian leader Pericles decided to rebuild many of the structures on the citys' chief fortress and sanctuary. The Parthenon was begun in 447 B.C. From anyones point of view, the columns of the temple appear to be straight, but in fact their built with a slight outward bulge. Its a subtle optical effect added for appearances sake. It works, too: one really cant tell that they arent straight. A huge amount of the Athenians's financial resources were used to rebuild the Parthenon, and to the Athenians it became a symbol of they're strength in the ancient world.

Quotation Marks

Activity 36-1

Using quotation marks correctly (See 36a-e.)

Edit the following passage, making sure that quotation marks are used correctly.

When I asked the director of the Center for Career Development what determines the kind of job a student gets after graduation, she replied, "Well, it depends on the type of student." "From my many years in this business, she said, I can say that students fall into different categories. She explained, "Some students are what I call "action students;" they jump right in and get involved with the center and keep using it until they find a really good job."Other students she defined as 'Micawbers.' (after the character in Dickens's David Copperfield who always expected things to turn out well for him without any effort on his part). These students think that their dream job will land in their lap, she said, and so they put off doing anything about finding it as long as possible As Donald Robert Perry Marquis so eloquently put it, 'Procrastination is the / art of keeping/ up with yesterday'." "To get them thinking about finding a job, we send out copies of articles they might find interesting, such as Campus Life's Tips on Landing a Great First Job.' and we encourage them to come in and meet us. Most of the Micawbers do eventually involve themselves in finding a job, but only after putting it off as long as possible, and few of them find the ideal job." A third kind of student she called "wanderers"; these never seek career guidance, and they continue to wander even once they are out of school. "Which one are you, and are you happy with your attitude?," she inquired.

Activity 36-2

Using quotation marks for brief, direct quotations (See 36a.)

Edit the following sentences, using quotation marks correctly with brief, direct quotations.

1. "Nice to see you, said the president. Sorry to be so disruptive."

2. He asked if any of the children read more than they watched TV. "At least they're honest," he said, taking note of the dearth of hands."

3. He comes through as someone who you'd like to coach your kid's Little League team," said one historian.

4. One critic said "that if Mr. Bush were reading a broad, soaring Kennedyesque speech with lots of overblown rhetoric, it would look like a suit that didn't fit, because it's not the way he speaks, and people don't believe he thinks like that."

5. Eli Attie said, "I don't agree with what his speeches say, but they're beautifully written, in a style" that Attie described as "plain spoken but high-minded, spare but elegant."

Activity 36-3

Using quotation marks for certain titles (See 36c.)

Edit the following sentences, using quotation marks correctly with titles. Circle the number of any sentence that is correct.

1. Jeff spent the evening reading "Lincoln at Gettysburg: The Words that Remade America," Garry Wills' definitive exegesis of "The Gettysburg Address."

2. Molly tried for the third time to make sense of "April Seventh, 1928," the opening chapter of Faulkner's The Sound and the Fury.

3. Sarah wrote her final college essay, Ishmael's Horizontal Sublime, Ahab's Vertical Sublime, a close examination of two major characters from Moby Dick.

4. Ben watched "Shadowball," an episode from the Ken Burns series Baseball.

5. Chad stayed in to study Thomas Hardy's poem At the Word 'Farewell.'

Activity 36-4

Using quotation marks for translations, specialized terms, ironic usages, and some nicknames (See 36d.)

Edit the following sentences, using quotation marks correctly with translations, specialized terms, ironic usages, and some nicknames.

1. Anyone can tell from their tofuburgers and sandals that Alice and Paul are the quintessential crunchy granolas.

2. They are easily persuaded by what is called green marketing, efforts by large corporations to convince consumers that their products are environmentally safe.

3. Their laid-back lifestyle probably comes from the fact that they live on the Left Coast, as California is sometimes called.

4. Since moving to California, their joie de vivre, or enjoyment of living, has increased greatly.

5. When they lived on the East Coast, Alice complained of feeling motivationally deficient, as the politically correct would say. In other words, she felt lazy.

Activity 36-5

Using other punctuation with quotation marks (See 36e.)

Edit the following sentences, adding quotation marks as needed and making sure that other punctuation marks are used correctly.

1. What you don't understand Dr. Burton explained, is that with animal research, we can test hypotheses and isolate variables. She sighed. Let me tell you about—she started to say.

2. I don't deny that animal research can yield valuable information, he interrupted. My problem is about whether it is morally defensible.

3. "Morally defensible!" she exclaimed. We're talking about saving lives! Because animal research leads to medical breakthroughs that benefit human beings, she added, I would call it a necessary evil.

4. "Just because we humans have a superior intellect, Sam suggested, does not mean that we should exploit less intelligent animals."

5. She replied I think we should draw a distinction not between more intelligent and less intelligent animals, but between human and nonhuman animals.

6. There is a distinction, Sam agreed. Humans are the only animals with a conscience. Knowing that, we should listen to that conscience, he added.

Activity 36-6

Avoiding misuses of quotation marks

Edit the following sentences by deleting misused quotation marks. If you are uncomfortable using a term without quotation marks, use a substitute term. Some sentences can be edited in more than one way. Circle the number of any sentence that is correct. For help, see box on p. 221 of *CWR*.

1. About three feet down the slope he lost his balance. After that, it was all "downhill."

2. Lance "Hotdog" Davies raced over toward the expert's slope and went flying down the supergiant slalom course.

3. Arnold should think about taking up golf instead of skiing. Then he won't get so "teed" off.

4. He tried bowling once, but he said it wasn't really up his "alley."

5. I don't know if I will be successful in persuading Arnold to give up skiing for baseball, but I'll give it my best "pitch."

Activity 36-7

> **Using quotation marks correctly**
>
> Edit the following passage to make sure that quotation marks and related punctuation are used correctly.

With the controversial election in 2000 of George W. Bush, many Americans were forced to consider the merits of the Electoral College. How can I believe that Mr. Bush is the president of the people when the majority of the people did not vote for him," said one bewildered Florida voter. Bush did win the "Electoral College," not the popular vote, thus spurring the controversy. But the controversy over the merits or demerits of the Electoral College is nothing new. It goes back to America's first-contested presidential election, in 1796, when John Adams edged Thomas Jefferson by three electoral votes. Since that initial controversy, which led Rep. William L. Smith of South Carolina to introduce the first constitutional amendment to reform the Electoral College, well over five hundred constitutional amendments to the process have been proposed. Some of our country's most notable public figures have endorsed an overhaul of the process: James Madison, Martin Van Buren, Andrew Jackson, Lyndon Johnson, Richard Nixon, Gerald Ford, and Hillary Clinton. Still, the Electoral College simply refuses to die, and it is unlikely that debate about it will either. One critic suggests that it is a national eccentricity" that gives us part of our national identity. "the Electoral College is to us what cricket is to the English, something that we know in our pores but can't explain to outsiders without making it more complicated than it already is." Out of this failure to communicate grows the sweet fruit of cultural pride."

Parentheses and Brackets

Activity 37-1

Using parentheses (See 37a.)

Edit the following sentences, inserting parentheses where appropriate and deleting parentheses that are unnecessary. You may need to make other changes in punctuation. Some sentences can be edited in more than one way.

1. In Europe, railroads were a major factor in the Industrial Revolution, see pp. 300–24.

2. England was the first country to open a public railroad, called "railway" by the British.

3. The first railroad to carry passengers began running in England in 1825–____?.

4. In some cases railroads grew on top of smaller tracks that were already in place in various industries, for example, in mining.

5. U.S. railroads were built to take advantage of the commerce and industry in the newly settled West, in those days Ohio was considered the West.

6. The rails were laid on wood, later concrete, cross ties (Modern railroads use continuous welded rails).

Activity 37-2

Using brackets (See 37b.)

Edit the following passage, using brackets correctly.

According to a 1997 study published in The New England Journal of Medicine collision rates for drivers using handheld cell phones were roughly the same as for drivers who were legally drunk. "There's no doubt that they (cell phones) can be a distraction to drivers," said one cell phone industry spokesperson. "But adjusting the radio can be just as dangerous," he added, "since they (drivers) must do two things at once just like using a cell phone." Another industry spokesperson remarked, "In most states accident reports filed by police don't reflect whether cell phones played a role (in causing accidents)." Clearly, industry executives would like to keep cause and effect relationship between cell phones and car accidents unproven and out of the public conversation. However, the recent car crash that left supermodel Nikki Taylor in critical condition has brought the issue of cell phone safety to national attention. (See the related article Taylor and the legal battles being fought to ban cell phones while driving (p. 16).)

Dashes, Slashes and Ellipsis Points

Activity 38-1

Using dashes (See 38a.)

Edit the following passage, inserting dashes wherever they are required.

The transcendentalist movement taking its name from a belief that was important in life transcended human comprehension flourished in New England in the mid-1800s. Its followers sought to bring together all kinds of people. Rich or poor, man or woman, old or young it didn't matter in the least to its proponents. The inspiration for the movement came from German idealists Kant in particular as well as from Eastern mystical philosophies. Its influence was felt in American literature Melville and Hawthorne's works, for example, and politics.

Activity 38-2

Using dashes (See 38a.)

Edit the following passage, deleting dashes where they are not effective. More than one edited version is possible.

John Steinbeck's novel—*East of Eden*—paints a symbolic re-creation of the Cain and Abel story—a story dealing with the nature of the conflict between good and evil. Caleb—Cain—and Aron—Abel are the sons of Adam Trask—representing both the biblical Adam and the Lord. Caleb—like Cain—wants the approval of his father. When Adam—the Father—rejects him, Caleb seeks revenge on Aron—just as Cain does to Abel. In the Bible, Cain kills Abel; in the novel, Caleb symbolically kills Aron—he destroys Aron's belief that their mother died a good woman—when in fact—she runs a legendary brothel that has made her a wealthy woman. Aron, unable to face the truth about his mother—joins the army and is killed. Unlike Cain—however—Caleb is not cast out of the land. Instead, he accepts responsibility for his brother's death.

Activity 38-3

Using ellipsis points (See 38b.)

Using ellipsis points, edit the following paragraph to shorten it for a paper on racism. More than one edited version is possible.

"Until we label an out-group it does not clearly exist in our minds. Take the curiously vague situation that we often meet when a person wishes to locate responsibility on the shoulders of some out-group whose nature he cannot specify. In such a case he usually employs the pronoun 'they' without an antecedent. 'Why don't they make these sidewalks wider?' 'I hear they are going to build a factory in this town and hire a lot of foreigners.' 'I won't pay this tax bill; they can just whistle for their money.' If asked 'who?' the speaker is likely to grow confused and embarrassed. The common use of the orphaned pronoun they teaches us that people often want and need to designate out-groups (usually for the purpose of venting hostility) even when they have no clear conception of the out-group in question. And so long as the target of wrath remains vague and ill-defined specific prejudice cannot crystallize around it. To have enemies we need labels."

Activity 38-4

Using parentheses, dashes, brackets, and slashes correctly

Edit the following passage, using parentheses, dashes, brackets, and slashes. More than one edited version is possible.

Lying close to the Statue of Liberty in New York Bay is tiny Ellis Island tiny in size but certainly not in importance. A single building occupies the island. Originally that building was a fort—1808—later an arsenal, and finally it took shape as we know it, an immigration station. Over a sixty-year period 1891—1954, officials at Ellis Island welcomed or, in many cases, rejected immigrants who had come from Europe to America the "melting pot" of the world's nations. The number of immigrants who came is staggering, more than twenty million, and most Americans today are either descended from or know someone who is descended from an Ellis Island immigrant. (My great-grandmother came through Ellis Island from Poland on 08/08/08. Although she was a very young child (four years old), she can clearly remember the experience.) For the arriving boatloads of Europeans, America's attractions were many, including a: freedom from persecution and b: the possibility of living a prosperous life. For a fictionalized account of one immigrant's arrival in America, read Mark Helprin's Ellis Island (Dell Publishers, 1982).

Activity 38-5

Using ellipsis points (See 38b.)

Using brackets (See 37b.)

The following passage is from an essay on Elvis Presley. Using ellipsis points and brackets as necessary, edit the passage as if you were going to quote from it in a formal research paper on popular culture in the American South. More than one edited version is possible.

Elvis was the most popular entertainer in the world, but nowhere as popular as in his native South. In the last years of his career, his audience in other parts of the country was generally centered in the original "fifties" fans whose youth and music were defined by Elvis, and in the lower or working class people who saw in Elvis some glamorized image of their own values. In the South, however, the pattern of Elvis's popularity tended to cut across age barriers and class lines which were themselves a less recognizable thing in a region which almost no one is more than a generation or two away from poverty, and where "class" in small communities might have more to do with family and past status than with money. Among Southern youth, Elvis was not a relic from a musical past; he was still one of the vital forces behind a Southern rock, which though different now from his, still echoes the rhythms which his music had fused out of the region.

Linda Ray Pratt, "Elvis, or the Ironies of Southern Identity"

Activity 38-6

Using parentheses, dashes, and brackets correctly

Edit the following paragraph, using parentheses, dashes, and brackets correctly. More than one edited version is possible.

When you're in the business of selling something, whether it be books or balloons you find out pretty quickly that the market isn't stationery (sic). That means you have to keep moving too. But how do you find new markets for your product? You should know from the outset that learning about them isn't easy for many reasons, such as the following: a: you might not have personal contacts for example, acquaintances to give you leads, b: you might not have much money for research, c: you might not be very knowledgeable about a certain area, and d: there might not be much information about them (new markets) when you start selling your product. There are thank goodness! a few things you can do to offset the difficulties, though. Keep up with the professional journals and handbooks there's a new one available every month, it seems. And remember to keep smiling, your biggest sale ever could be right around the corner!

Spelling

Activity 39-1

Editing for spelling errors (See 39a-b.)

Edit the following passage, making sure there are no misspelled words.

Most college instructors have a very prejudice view of human intelligence. They basicly define intelligence as the ability to solve complex mathmatical problems or to conduct origanal research in labratories or to express complicated ideas in writting. Students can "prove" there intelligence only by getting high marks in as many subjects as possble. However, knowledgable psychologists have begun to view human intelligence alot more broadly then before, and they now believe that many diffrent kinds of intelligence may be studied and measured all by themselfs with new tests and methods. According to this arguement, for example, artistic ability is a special kind of intelligence, present from berth, that allows a person to percieve reality in a way that other people can not and then to translate those perceptions into unique phyzical forms. Excellence at foot ball and other sports requirs another kind of intelligence that many researchers guess is largly unconscience but that still involves speciallized mental abilities present even in babys. If even athaletes could be reconized for there inborn intelligence, the affect on education would be truely revolutionary.

Activity 39-2

Checking for commonly confused words (See 39a.)

Edit the following poem, correcting the homonyms and similar-sounding words that are misused.

Spell Checker

Eye halve a spelling chequer

It came with my pea sea

It plainly marques four my revue

Miss steaks eye kin knot sea.

Eye strike a key and type a word

And weight four it two say

Weather eye am wrong oar write

It shows me strait a weigh.

As soon as a mist ache is maid

It nose bee fore two long

And eye can put the error rite

Its rare lea ever wrong.

Eye have run this poem threw it

I am shore your pleased two no

Its letter perfect awl the weigh

My chequer tolled me sew.

Activity 39-3

Using basic spelling rules (See 39b.)

Edit the following passage, using basic spelling rules to eliminate misspelled words.

Early in my senior year of high school, I had to make the very touch decision about where I wanted to go to college. I sent away for brochures and catalogs from a number of schools, and when I received the, I leaved threw them to get some ideas of colleges that offered programs in the engineering field. I was hoping to get into one of the colleges or universitys in the Midwest, specificly in the state of Michigan. I looked into attendding the University of Michigan, and I saw that it had quite an extensive engineering program. I have an aunt who majored in mechanical engineering at the University of Michigan, so she is very knowledgable about the program. She told me that it is basicly a very good program, but that it is also a lot of work. The curriculum offers many different courses leading to a bachelor of science degree. Some of the major subjects are design, solid and fluid mechanics, manufactureing processes and systems, and thermodynamics. In addition to these courses, six courses in the humanitys and social sceince feilds are required. After considerring it for a week, I decided that the University of Michigan was where I would go to get my college education.

Capitalization

Activity 40-1

Editing for correct capitalization (See 40a-e.)

Edit the following passage for problems with capitalization.

My family lived in Yeehaw for two years (It seemed more like a century), and while we were there my Sister Joy and I attended Franklin senior high school. The building was a run-down three-story structure that looked like it had barely survived World war II. It was about a mile South of our house on Joel street, and although we could have taken the bus, on our first day of school Joy said, "let's avoid contact for as long as possible," so we got into the habit of walking.

From early Fall through christmas of that year, we tried to make the best of what we both agreed was a bad situation. The principal was fat and bald, wore Cowboy boots and a string tie, and called the boys "Pardners" and the girls "Little ladies."Our English teacher was like a dr. seuss character; she was tall with a long thin neck and hair that stood straight up on her head, and she introduced herself the first day of class by saying, "My name is mrs. Hamm. Mrs. Hamm I am."We sent the first six weeks reading Romeo And Juliet, which according to her had two main shakespearean themes:(1) young people living during the renaissance talked a lot better than young people today. (2) It never pays to listen to a catholic priest.

Activity 40-2

Capitalizing the first word of a sentence (See 40a.)

Edit the following passage, using a capital letter at the beginning of every sentence or deliberate sentence fragment. More than one edited version is possible.

Why do some people become addicts while others do not? Does it have to do with genetics? personality types? environmental factors? Some behavioral scientists believe that alcoholics are particular personality types. Long-term studies indicate that specific personality traits show up early in life:Children who are impulsive and easily distracted might, for instance, turn into addicts later in life. (of course, some impulsive, easily distracted children do not become addicts.) Not all scientists ascribe to the personality-type theory, however. Another group believes that the answer lies in the following area: The study of genetic indicators. These scientists engage in studies on identical twins, hoping to shed light on who is at risk of becoming an addict.

Activity 40-3

Capitalizing quotations and lines of poetry (See 40b.)

Edit the following passage to make capitalization in quotations correct.

"It feels really cold," Susan said, bending down to dip her hand into the water. "And it's only September."

"Poor Champ!" Dan replied. "he must be freezing."

"Who?" Susan asked. "who's Champ? What are you talking about?"

"Don't tell me you've never heard of Champ!" Dan said in disbelief. "He's Lake Champlain's answer to the Loch Ness monster."

"Are you pulling my leg,"Susan inquired,"Or is this for real?"

"It's real,"Dan said. "I swear! You've never heard any of the stories about a sea serpent living in this lake? Dozens of people have reported seeing him. Samuel de Champlain wrote about him first," he explained. "in his log, he described a giant sea serpent with bubble eyes, horns on his head, and a round barrel body."

"So now I'm supposed to believe that not only is there a mysterious creature in the lake," Susan said skeptically, "But that this creature has been alive for nearly four hundred years! How gullible do you think I am?"

"It's not the same creature," Dan replied. "obviously there has been more than one Champ. I can see that you still don't believe me. Let's go over to the library and you can read the articles for yourself."

"All right,"Susan replied, "But you'll never convince me that he is real."

Activity 40-4

Capitalizing proper nouns and their derivatives (See 40c.)

Edit the following sentences, correcting the capitalization of nouns and their derivatives.

1. Nixon's opponent in the november election was senator George McGovern from south Dakota.

2. Attorney general John Mitchell ran Nixon's campaign.

3. One year before the 1972 election, the twenty-sixth amendment had given eighteen-year-olds the right to vote.

4. The scandal that led to president Nixon's downfall is known as watergate. It is named after the office building where the democratic national committee had its Headquarters.

5. The President abused his Presidential powers by using Government Agencies, such as the federal bureau of investigation and the CIA, to spy on people.

6. In the midst of the Watergate investigations during the Fall of 1973, war broke out in the middle east on yom kippur.

7. Investigators proved that the republican abuses involved many Agencies, including the cia, fbi, and the irs.

8. During the televised senate investigation, millions of americans—from the big apple to L.A.—were glued to their television sets.

9. The investigation gripped the viewers' attention, much like the iran-contra hearings or the confirmation of supreme court justice Clarence Thomas

10. Members of the U.S. congress were prepared to impeach Nixon, but he resigned before they could do so.

Activity 40-5

Capitalizing titles of books and other works (See 40d.)

Edit the following sentences by correctly capitalizing all titles.

1. In my research on Abraham Lincoln, I discovered an interesting book about his wife—the Insanity File: The Case Of Mary Todd Lincoln.

2. Director Spike Lee based the script for his film Malcolm x on the book The autobiography of Malcolm X.

3. George Bernard Shaw considered Euripides the greatest of the Greek dramatists. The plays of Euripides that are most famous include Medea and Electra. Lesser known plays include Iphigenia Among the Taurians, The Bacchants, and Iphigenia at Aulis.

4. Dorothy Parker won the distinguished O. Henry Award for her short story "Big blonde," which was included in her 1933 collection, After such Pleasures. She also wrote screenplays, winning an Oscar for a Star is Born.

5. In 1967 Jonathan Kozol won the National Book Award for his first book, Death at An Early Age. With books such as Savage Inequities: Children In America's Schools (1991) and Amazing Grace: the Lives of Children and The Conscience of a Nation (1995), Kozol became one of the most eloquent advocates for children in America.

Activity 40-6

Using capital letters correctly

Edit the following passage, using capital letters according to the guidelines in this chapter.

The renaissance, a term that means "rebirth," began in italy in the mid-fourteenth century and spread throughout western Europe by the middle of the sixteenth century. and what a time of rebirth! With the help of numerous patrons of the arts, such as the Medici Family in Florence, learning, literature, and the arts flourished. Lorenzo de' Medici was the influential patron of the great artist Botticelli, whose works include The birth of Venus and La primavera.(the works of Botticelli became great favorites of the Pre-Raphaelites.)

The pursuit of literature and the arts was also fostered by Popes, such as Pope Nicholas V. Petrarch and Boccaccio were among the first writers to become interested in secular literature. Before the renaissance, most of the literature read in their christian society had been related to the church. During the Renaissance, an interest in reading latin and greek literature grew, and many people put their energy into collecting manuscripts, often ransacking monastic libraries throughout europe to obtain them. Countless old manuscripts are now housed in many of the great museums and libraries of the world, including the British museum.

The Renaissance was also a turning point in philosophy and science. Galileo and Copernicus, for example, made great discoveries in the field of astronomy.

Hyphens

Activity 41-1

Using hyphens correctly (See 41a-d.)

Edit the following passage making sure that all words are hyphenated correctly.

Government expenditures for education have mush-roomed, tripling since 1982 to a staggering $17.2 billion in 2000. Despite this substantial financial backing, test scores in math and reading have remained flat. Considering that the continued increase in federal funding has apparently yielded little improvement in student learning, it is no wonder that education reform has become a bi-partisan issue for the new millennium. But before reformminded Democrats and Republicans tackle the problems of education, they must define "reform." While both parties agree with the idea to "leave no child behind," they dis-agree on how to accomplish it. This is due in-part to how each views federal spending on education. Both parties have been at odds on how much money the federal government should pitch in and how that money should be used. Republicans argue that the Clinton era notion of reform was a self defeating cycle that saw the federal government continually pour money into education and have little to show for it. They call for some restraint on spending for education-reform and place emphasis on testing and accountability. Some Democrats agree to an extent. One Democratic senator said, ``I'm all in favor of a modest federal role [in education], but I don't want that to mature into a fullfledged un-funded mandate.'' But some Democrats question whether a Republican plan provides enough money to adequately support states to develop necessary tests. Furthermore, Democrats want more money to repair schools and hire teachers. Once the parties reach a compromise, they should realize that a carefully-developed plan would be the only way to provide meaningful education reform for America's children.

Activity 41-2

Hyphenating words at the ends of lines (See 41a.)

Indicate the best place for hyphenating each of the following words. Not all words should be hyphenated. You may want to use a dictionary to check your hyphenation.

1. coordinated
2. acquitted
3. preparedness
4. width
5. crossbones

6. minibus
7. ignite
8. overcast
9. commitment
10. antidote

Activity 41-3

Hyphenating words at the ends of lines (See 41a.)

Indicate the best place for hyphenating each of the following words. If a word contains more than two syllables, indicate all possible hyphenation points. Not all words should be hyphenated. You may want to use a dictionary to check your hyphenation.

1. wrecked
2. macroeconomics
3. enough
4. preamble
5. counterbalance

6. recessed
7. eavesdrop
8. discernment
9. reunification
10. against

Activity 41-4

Hyphenating after some prefixes (See 41b.)

Hyphenating to link parts of compound words (See 41c.)

Edit the following sentences, using hyphens when necessary and deleting unnecessary hyphens.

1. The new mayor is a selfassured woman whose attitude is strongly pro business.
2. The above mentioned former mayor re-ceived very few votes from pre or post-retirement voters.
3. Many people criticized him for supposedly unAmerican ideas and for his lack of support for the Canada U.S. trade agreement.
4. The new mayor hopes to recreate jobs in the inner city.
5. She plans to re-vive industry and bring pro-ductivity to pre-existing levels.
6. Skeptics doubt that her plan will lead to the re-covery she has promised.
7. Her team of socalled experts is not well-regarded by the former mayor's advisers.
8. She expects to restore the city to pre 1980 levels of prosperity.
9. If the economy re-covers, more people will be self sufficient.
10. At his farewell address, the exmayor ex-pressed his desire to reenter politics someday.

Activity 41-5

Hyphenating in fractions, numbers, and units of measure (See 41d.)

Edit the following sentences to make sure that all fractions, numbers, and units of measure are hyphenated correctly.

1. Each team member runs for 150-200 miles in a season.

2. Two thirds of the team also competed last year.

3. The youngest runner, a seventeen year-old, thinks she can beat last year's champion, who is nineteen years old.

4. The coach insists on a ninety minute practice every day.

5. The team's best time is in the 60 yard dash.

Activity 41-6

Using hyphens correctly (See 41a-d.)

Edit the following passage, hyphenating all words where necessary and deleting unnecessary hyphens. You may have to consult a dictionary.

Last year's Super Bowl was dominated by numerous dot-com and e commerce commercials. In sharp contrast, the 2001 Super Bowl featured only two commercials from the high tech industry. This contrast reflected the steep drop in technology-stock prices that occurred in April 2000. Prior to this date the prosperity gained from high-tech stocks seemed neverending. So what happened? The decline in high-tech stocks resulted in post-ponements of public stock offerings, which in the past had been a fool-proof way to raise cash for start up Internet companies. Venture capitalists had been willing to pour big money into these companies because they could re-cover their investments through a soaring stock market, selling their stock for much more than they had paid for it. However, when high-tech stock began to decline, venture capitalists became overly-cautious about investing in start up companies that had no profits in sight. A ripple-effect was felt by employees of Internet firms. The long term compensation of many of these employees was tied to their stock options in their respective firms. These employees didn't need to watch the 2001 Super Bowl to begin feeling the longlasting effects of a good market gone bad.

Numbers

Activity 42-1

Using numbers appropriately (See 42a-b.)

Edit the following passage to make sure that all numbers are handled appropriately.

It is hard to believe, but our present-day popcorn has roots going back at least five thousand six hundred years in the american Southwest and over 75 thousand years in Central and South America. A staple food in many early cultures, popcorn is now the most popular prepared snack food in the United States: it is estimated that as many as 2, 000, 000 bags are sold daily in movie theatres alone, representing just 1/8 of the total amount eaten.

Having smelled the aroma of popping corn wafting from local dorm rooms as early as 7 o'clock in the morning (and as late as four-thirty A.M.), my roommate and I decided to conduct an informal poll to see how popular popcorn is on campus. 70 students participated in our survey, which we conducted in front of the library for 2 1/2 hours a day over five days (the week of March thirteenth, 1992). Of the respondents, forty-eight percent were women and fifty-two percent were men, and the average age was twenty-two. Our questionnaire consisted of 12 questions (see Appendix A).

Activity 42-2

Using numbers for non-technical writing (See 42b.)

Edit the following passage, making sure all numbers are handled appropriately for non-technical writing.

1. When he was 15, Christian Jacq became fascinated with Eygptology.
2. He went on to earn his doctorate in Egyptian studies from the Sorbonne and published several serious histories. In nineteen eighty-seven, his first successful
   novel was published.
3. But it was his 5-volume biographical epic about Ramses II, the pharaoh who ruled Egypt from 1279 to 1213 BC, which caused a sensation in the publishing industry.
4. 100s of fans lined up outside of bookstores as each new volume was released, and by two thousand the popular series had sold eleven million copies in 29 countries.
5. The Ramses series also spurred a one hundred % increase in the number of French tourists traveling to Egypt.
6. Jacq's latest series, The Stone of Light, had an initial printing of 1.5 million copies and was available in twenty-two languages.

Activity 42-3

Using numbers for non-technical writing (See 42b.)

Edit the following sentences, writing out numbers or using figures according to convention for non-technical writing. Circle the number of any sentence that is correct.

1. In 2/3 of the states, math scores rose dramatically.

2. Increases in scores for verbal aptitude ranged from 2.6% to twenty-eight percent.

3. In one high school in the Northwest, ten students scored higher than 750 on the math test, 125 scored between 550 and 750, and 40 scored below 550.

4. The average age of the students who participated was sixteen.

5. The first part of the test began at nine A.M. and ended at 9:45.

6. Ninety-five percent of the schools reported their scores on time.

7. Statisticians pored over the 40,000 tests, analyzing data for 13 days.

8. An analysis of the results of the survey can be found on page twelve of today's newspaper.

9. The testing took place on October twelfth, 1992, and February eighteenth, 1993.

Abbreviations

Activity 43-1

Using abbreviations correctly (See 43a-g.)

Edit the following passage to make sure that abbreviations have been used according to the guidelines in this chapter.

The legendary Blue Angels, the U.S. Navy's flight demonstration squadron, headlined Air Expo '01 at the Patuxent River Naval Air Station this past Fri. and Sat. On both days at 2:45 pm sharp, the take off of "Fat Albert," a C-130 Hercules, signified the start of the Blue Angels' show. Eight solid-fuel rocket bottles thrust the Hercules skyward. Fired simultaneously and burning for appx. fourteen sec., the jet-assisted takeoff bottles allow "Fat Albert" to reach an alt. of one thousand ft. in short order. At 3:00 P.M. sharp, the Angels made their entrance to the delight of the eager audience. With clear skies and seventy degree weather, the day was perfect for both the audience and the Angels. For over an hr. the six Blue Angel pilots, each with well over 1,350 flight hrs., thrilled the crowd with precision flying. The team illustrated a variety of high-speed, low-altitude maneuvers, locked as a unit in the renowned, six-jet Delta Formation. Captain Patrick Hovatter, commanding officer of the base, said the next performance of the Blue Angels would be in Dec. at Andrews Air Force Base, just outside of Washington, District of Columbia.

Activity 43-2

Using abbreviations correctly (See 43a-g.)

Edit the following passage, using abbreviations as appropriate.

Although the United States Constitution is supposed to guarantee equal rights to all people regardless of color, in the first half of this century most African Americans in the southern U.S. lived in deplorable conditions. E.g., African Americans had to use separate washrooms, and they could not attend school with whites. Not until the 1940s did the United States Supreme Court finally begin to outlaw practices that deprived African Americans of their rights. One small step toward equality was made when representatives from the National Association for the Advancement of Colored People (N.A.A.C.P.) persuaded the Court that maintaining separate schools for African Americans and whites was not equal. In 1954, under Chief Justice Earl Warren of Calif., the Court ordered the desegregation of schools in the U.S. Despite the new legislation, however, the southern states still resisted integration, and only Senator Lyndon Johnson from TX and two sen. from Tenn. (Estes Kefauver and Albert Gore, Senior) were in favor of desegregating the schools. Racial conflict raged throughout the southern states over the issue of integration; one area of conflict was Little Rock, Ark., where resistance was so great that the National Guard had to be used to enforce integration. Even this drastic step did not solve the problem, however, and the struggle for equal education and other civil rights for African Americans went on for many years.

Activity 43-3

Using abbreviations correctly (See 43a-g.)

Edit the following sentences, making sure that abbreviations are used correctly. Circle the number of any sentence that is correct.

1. Prof. Smithers started the co-op because he was frustrated by the devastating effects of the recession.

2. Neighborhood residents line up outside the co-op around 6:00 A.M.

3. Whether it is 95° Fahrenheit or -15° Fahrenheit, there is always a long line of hungry people.

4. Next Sat., the mayor will visit the co-op. Mayor Ruth Brown has been a supporter of the co-op from the beginning.

5. The number of households receiving food stamps has increased 25 percent in the past two years.

6. Since unemployment has risen 3% in the past year, it is not surprising that the number of people requiring assistance has also risen.

7. When the co-op first opened, Senator Lillian Good held a news conference to increase public awareness of poverty.

8. With an annual budget of 60,000 dollars, the co-op is the main source of food for the community's low-income residents.

9. Each household receives two gal. of milk every week.

10. As part of his fundraising efforts, Dr. Smithers, Ph.D., has requested donations from local businesses.

11. Donations to the co-op may be sent to 34 N. Branch St., Willowdale, Ohio 44667.

Italics and Underlining

Activity 44-1

Using italics correctly (See 44a-d.)

Edit the following passage to make sure that words are italicized according to the guidelines of this chapter.

The Sex Life of Flowers, a book by Bastiaan Meeuse and Sean Morris, originated as an episode broadcast on public television's "Nature" series under the title Sexual Encounters of the Floral Kind. Like the documentary, the book is a fascinating look at the many unusual adaptations plants have made in order to achieve pollination. In Chapter 2, The Flower, the authors report that pollination among flowering plants (known by the biological term angiosperms) is generally an act of quid pro quo; that is, in order to get something (the pollen-carrying services of bees and other insects), flowers must give something in return (usually food, in the form of nectar). Consequently, flowers have developed shapes and colors designed to attract visitors to a rendezvous with the nectar inside. For example in the forget-me-not flower (Myosotis palustris), a bright yellow ring surrounds and highlights the dark entrance; the meadow cranesbill (Geranium pratense) offers a similar contrast by reflecting no ultraviolet light from the flower center. Like the male and female of other species, flowers and insects must be simpatico if the process of reproduction is to take place.

Activity 44-2

Using italics correctly (See 44a.)

Edit the following sentences, using italic (and quotation marks) according to the guidelines in this chapter.

1. E. B. White's essay, Once More to the Lake, originally appeared in One Man's Meat, his column for Harper's Magazine.

2. White, a writer and editor for "The New Yorker," also wrote the beloved children's classic, "Charlotte's Web," which was later turned into an animated film.

3. One of White's closest friends at "The New Yorker" was humorist James Thurber, whose own writings also made it to the big screen. "The Secret Life of Walter Mitty" was the film version of a Thurber short story by the same title, and the 1969 television series, My World and Welcome to It, took its name from a Thurber book.

4. Garrison Kellior, radio host of "A Prairie Home Companion" and author of Lake Wobegon Days, paid tribute to Thurber by editing a collection of the humorist's writings and cartoons.

5. Like Keillor, it was in radio that another humorist Jean Shepard found his true voice. In the words of media critic Marshall McLuhan, Shepard was "the first radio novelist." Strauss's "The Gallop" signaled the start of Shepard's WOR radio broadcasts.

Activity 44-3

Italicizing the names of individual trains, ships, airplanes, and spacecraft (See 44b.)

Italicizing foreign words (See 44c.)

Edit the following sentences, using italics as necessary. Delete any unnecessary italics. You may need to check a dictionary for some terms. Circle the number of any sentence that is correct.

1. Along the way she passed many different kinds of trees, including Quercus alba, Acer rubrum, and Abies balsamea.

2. The "Adirondack," Amtrak's day train to Montreal, is fine, but the night train is the crème de la crème.

3. While in Montreal, Louise visited museums and galleries and admired many wonderful objets d'art.

4. In a little French café in the old part of the city, Louise ordered pâté, hors d'oeuvres, and vin de Bordeaux rouge. She tried not to make a faux pas when ordering.

5. One day she went on a boat tour up the St. Lawrence River on the "Pride of Montreal." Unfortunately, because of the choppy waters, she suffered from mal de mer.

6. Louise is a bit of a bon vivant:She adores le boire et le manger in Montreal.

7. When it was time to leave, Louise sighed and said, "Tempus fugit—especially when you're having fun."

Activity 44-4

Italicizing for emphasis (See 44d.)

Edit the following sentences, making sure that italics are used correctly for words presented as words and for emphasis. Circle the number of any sentence that is correct.

1. Expressionism is characterized by a revolt against realism.

2. In expressionist literature, authors represent the world not objectively, but rather subjectively—as it appears to them.

3. Expressionist painters often used intense colors and simple forms to convey strong emotions.

4. Surrealism is the name given to a movement that began in France around the same time as expressionism began in Germany.

5. Surrealists owed much to the work of Freud; they emphasized dreams, fantasy, and the power of the unconscious over the conscious mind.

6. The term literature of the absurd is given to works founded on the belief that the human condition is essentially absurd.

7. Literature of the absurd has its roots in the movements of expressionism and surrealism.

Activity 44-5

    Using italics correctly (See 44a-d.)

    Edit the following passage, making sure words are italicized appropriately.

    Before planting a garden it is a good idea to consult a reputable source for tips on successful gardening. Many newspapers, such as the New York Times, have a weekly column devoted to gardening. There are also many useful books, such as "A Guide to Growing Gorgeous Greenery," with its especially useful introductory chapter, Plan before You Plant.

    First a gardener should learn about the different types of plants. Annuals is the term given to plants that complete their lifetime in one year; the term perennials is used for plants that grow back every year: Many annuals are poplar with gardeners, especially the Begonia semperflorens and the Petunia hybrida.

    Another issue for gardeners to consider is pesticides. Environmentally conscious gardeners are not opposed to pesticides per se, but they use only organc pesticides, which derive from natural rather than synthetic substances. Gardening books are useful sans doute, and they may prevent the worst faux pas in the garden, but in the end there is no one way to make a garden—chacun à son goût!

Fragment Sentences

Activity 45-1

Eliminating sentence fragments (See 45a-c.)

Edit the following passage to eliminate sentence fragments. More than one edited version is possible.

My experience as a camp counselor has taught me many lessons. The kind of lessons I cannot easily put into words. For two summers now I have worked as a counselor at a camp for children with learning disabilities. Each summer the entire staff gathers for a week of training at the end of June. After a few weeks of recovering from finals and the end of school. This training period is important. Because there is a lot to keep in mind when working with these children. Learning disabilities can be triggered by a long list of causes. Such as behavioral problems, visual or perceptual difficulties, or the strain of an unhappy life at home. To name just a few. That first week of training helps the counseling staff to keep these possible causes in mind and to be more sensitive to the problems each individual child might face.

I will always remember one nine-year-old boy named Johnny. Who was a camper during my first summer as a counselor. Johnny had trouble reading even the simplest sentences aloud. Every time he tried to read aloud his whole body would grow tense. And he would stumble painfully over every word. One day before reading class I had an idea. When it was Johnny's turn to read that day, I sat beside him. Gently rubbing his back as he began to read. It worked. Johnny's body relaxed, and he read an entire paragraph with only a few stumbles. When he finished he looked up at me with wide, surprised eyes. And grinned from ear to ear.

Activity 45-2

Recognizing and editing phrase fragments (see 45a.)

Edit the following passage to eliminate any fragments, making small changes in wording or punctuation that are necessary for smooth reading. More than one edited version is possible.

Sally had the most peculiar look on her face. As she began to poke into the tank for a lobster. With her entire arm about to become wet and her heart racing. She couldn't believe her first date with Sam started at a lobster shack. Sal's Shack whose motto was "You pick 'em, we cook 'em." Boasted an atmosphere that could only be described as "beyond laid back." She wondered why Sam failed to tell her the appropriate clothes to wear. Shorts, tee-shirt, and sandals. Her silk blouse and suede pants seemed completely out of place. Until a beautiful woman, in her mid-forties, dressed in a stunning evening dress, grabbed her hand and said, "Hi. I'm Sam's mom, Sal. You must be Sally. We come from a long line of practical jokers. There's a formal dining area is in the back. This area is just for the beach crowd." Sally's peculiar look melted into one of relief.

Activity 45-3

Recognizing and editing dependent clause fragments (see 45a.)

Edit the following paragraph to eliminate dependent clause fragments. More than one edited version is possible.

Despite the fact that doctors take an oath to protect life. Many physicians believe they should be allowed to help patients who want to commit suicide. They want to do whatever they can to ease the pain of death for those who are suffering. Because they believe people should be able to die with dignity. In Europe, although euthanasia is not legal, it is becoming more accepted in some countries, such as the Netherlands. Which has one of the most liberal policies in the world. There, specific guidelines allow a doctor to assist in the suicide of a patient who is terminally ill. As long as the patient requests it.

Activity 45-4

Eliminating sentence fragments (See 45a-c)

Edit the following passage to eliminate sentence fragments. Make any small changes in wording that are needed for smooth reading. More than one edited version is possible.

Ferninand le Menthe Morton was born in New Orleans to a Creole family. Although he took classical piano lessons, he fell in love with another kind of music. Jazz and blues. Which he heard in the part of town called Storyville. In Chicago in the 1920s, he got a recording contract with RCA. He made some records and began calling himself "Jelly Roll." He claimed to have invented jazz. By himself. George G. Wolfe wrote a musical about his life. Called Jelly's Last Jam and written as though looking back from the moment of his death.

At the end of his life, Morton came face to face with the contributions of other blacks to jazz. Which he had denied all his life. He also had to confront the heritage he shared with black musicians. He eventually came to accept and understand them. Although he had always thought of himself, a Creole, as different from blacks.

Comma Splices and Fused Sentences

Activity 46-1

Eliminating fused sentences and comma splices (See 46a-f.)

Edit the following passage to eliminate fused sentences and comma splices. More than one edited version is possible.

Historians have made us aware that the Iroquois Indians of the northeastern United States had a form of government very much like the democracies of today however few people are aware of the important roles played by women in the Iroquois tribes. Iroquois women held important rights and responsibilities in many areas, including political life, social life, civil decisions, religious ceremonies, and land rights. Iroquois women had an important voice in public councils, they were free to make nominations just as the men were. Within the family, the Iroquois woman played roles still played by men in many cultures, she negotiated marriages and governed the household. The Iroquois mother had certain maternal rights. For example, it was up to the mother of a particular clan to decide which of the offspring would carry on the clan title. Similarly, the Iroquois woman held possession of lands and properties she could bequeath them to whomever she chose. In the case of civil decisions such as clan disputes over land, Iroquois women held important responsibilities. They acted as modern-day judges do, they ruled on who held rights to land and property. And finally, in religious life Iroquois women played important roles in various festivals and ceremonies. Some cultures still deny fundamental rights to women, years and years ago the Iroquois Indians were calling the earth their "mighty mother" and treating women with respect.

Activity 46-2

Using a comma and a coordinating conjunction (see 46a.)

Edit each fused sentence or comma splice using a comma and a coordinating conjunction. More than one editing option is available to you.

1. The praise that David Halberstam has received for his nonfiction writing is due in large part to his blunt style he always says what he means.

2. He was critical of the media's involvement in the 1988 presidential election, he said so openly.

3. In his writing he not only identifies the point he is tryng to make, he also proceeds to solidify and clarify it.

4. He leads the reader through his thought processes, rarely is any point unsubstantiated.

5. He feels strongly about his subjects he seems to become very involved with them.

Activity 46-3

Using a semicolon (See 46b.)

Edit each fused sentence or comma splice using either a semicolon alone or a semicolon with a conjunctive adverb or transitional expression. More than one editing option is available to you.

1. Scientist Francis Collins possesses an impressive record of discovery in the field of genetics, he discovered the gene that causes cystic fibrosis and was the lead researcher in finding the genes that cause neurofibromatosis and Huntington chorea.

2. Such groundbreaking discoveries suggest a strong educational background, Collins holds an M.S. and a Ph.D. from Yale and an M.D. from the University of North Carolina at Chapel Hill.

3. His degrees from these prestigious institutions offer an interesting contrast to his early education, Collins was homeschooled by his mother for much of his young life.

4. Collins maintains a sincere desire to help humanity through successful research, in fact, he took a sizable pay cut to lead the government-backed Human Genome Project.

5. Collins clearly understood the moral and ethical implications of unraveling the human genetic map, in congressional hearings he urged the passage of federal law to set guidelines on how individuals' genetic information could be handled.

Activity 46-4

Using a colon (See 46c.)

Edit each fused sentence or comma splice using a colon.

1. Ben and Jerry are known for their support of environmental causes, they recycle their plastic spoons and all recyclable paper trash.

2. The company is "one percent for peace," one percent of all sales goes toward supporting peacekeeping efforts worldwide.

3. They have an innovative way of generating business from time to time they give out free ice cream.

4. Ben and Jerry's is a great place to work, the co-workers are friendly, and sometimes employees get to take home free ice cream.

5. Ben and Jerry sought a location for their factory that would meet their specific demands, easy access to transportation, fresh water, and a high-quality work force were all important factors.

Activity 46-5

Using a semicolon (See 46d.)

Edit each fused sentence or comma splice by separating it into two sentences.

1. Thurgood Marshall, one of the most important figures in twentieth-century American life, died in 1993 he was eighty-four years old.

2. Marshall gained recognition from the 1954 Supreme Court decision Brown v. Board of Education, it was a landmark in American history.

3. Not everyone was happy with the decision that put an end to the "separate but equal" system of racial segregation, much turmoil followed.

4. Marshall was excluded from the all-white law school that later honored him, they named the library after him.

5. America was deep in the Great Depression when Marshall began his career as a lawyer times were very tough economically.

Activity 46-6

Subordinating one clause to the other (See 46c.)

Edit the following passage to eliminate fused sentences and comma splices by subordinating clauses as appropriate. More than one edited version is possible.

Darkness falls the animals begin to settle down for the night. The horses all have their favorite places to sleep, they sleep standing. The chickens have already settled into the shed, occasionally they give off a muffled coo. The piglets playfully scampered all day now they lie quietly in a comfortable pile in the corner of their pen. Everything is quiet, little scratching, scurrying sounds can be heard from the feed room. The mice have come out, they believe they are the true owners of the barn. To a mouse a barn must resemble a cornucopia of hay, oats, and other delicacies, its other residents are all messy eaters. Three of the mice gnaw at the corner of a sack of rolled oats. The three are thinking of nothing but oats around the corner of the door creeps the cat.

Activity 46-7

Rewriting the sentences as one independent clause (See 46f.)

Edit each fused sentence or comma splice by making it a single independent clause. More than one editing option is available to you.

1. Hamlet is the most popular of Shakespeare's plays, more has been written about it than any other drama.

2. Shakespeare fused several similar plots, he created a new one that is just a little different.

3. One theme in the play is revenge another used is madness.

4. A third theme is crisis, it is created in the play by Hamlet's mother through her sin with Hamlet's uncle.

5. All three themes are familiar ones Shakespeare's blending of them makes them fascinating.

Activity 46-8

Eliminating fused sentences and comma splices (See 45a-f.)

Edit the following passage to eliminate fused sentences and comma splices using any strategy discussed in this chapter.

In the good ole days, all you needed to draw a crowd were a grass diamond, peanuts, dogs and beer, and two professional ball clubs. The baseball stadiums of the future will provide so much more, they offer video kiosks, gourmet food, luxury suites, learning centers, meeting rooms, and retractable roofs and since 1991 these new stadiums have led the way to baseball's resurgence. Since 1991 ten new facilities have opened. Camden Yards, which opened in 1992, led the way, winning national awards and high praise from both fans and architecture critics alike. Located smack in the middle of downtown Baltimore, Camden Yards hearkened back to the urban stadium of old with its brick façade, natural grass, and advertising in old-fashioned lettering. Such was the success of Camden that many major league cities followed suite, Jacobs Field in Cleveland, Coors Field in Denver, The Ballpark at Arlington (Texas), and Turner Field in Atlanta all incorporated the classic and contemporary design elements featured at Camden. However, architects may be expanding this "retro" style of building stadiums this expanded vision will include much more: food courts with name-brand outlets, restaurants, stores selling team products, batting cages, swimming pools, tanning decks, hot tubs, and more. Stadiums of the new millennium will more than likely resemble theme parks like Disney World, they sure won't just resemble a place with bleachers, hot dogs, peanuts, and beer.

Unnecessary Shifts and Mixed Constructions

Activity 47-1

Eliminating unnecessary shifts or mixed constructions (See 47a-h.)

Edit the following passage to make all sentences consistent and complete by eliminating any unnecessary shifts or mixed constructions. More than one edited version is possible.

We tend to think of technological change and the dangers it poses as problems unique to our time. But there has always been technological growth of some kind, and always that growth will bring unexpected pitfalls. Can we imagine, for instance, that the Pyramids, the great Gothic cathedrals, the Roman viaducts, and the Great Wall of China were built without unfortunate incidents or injuries to the workers? In early America, improvements in home heating apparatuses, new building techniques and materials, and closer placement of houses as towns grew larger and larger. All these things led to frequent unmanageable fires now would start and spread more easily. In time, the coping mechanism of fire houses and trained fire fighters were devised and implemented. Later on, steamboat travel was all the rage. But the steam engines were prone to explosions. In one five-year period, 270 deaths resulted in such explosions. The government finally stepped in to insisted on safer designs. Train travel brought newly hazardous. At one point, twenty-five railroad bridges were collapsing every year. What is comforting is where society has found safeguards against so many of these life-threatening perils. We have learned from centuries of mistakes; maybe humanity will eventually learn to anticipate the threats our progress can pose.

Activity 47-2

Avoiding unnecessary shifts (See 47a–e.)

Edit the following sentences to avoid distracting or awkward shifts. Some sentences have more than one possible answer.

1. The entire freshman class did well on their exam.

2. We were given one hour for the examination, and do not use any books.

3. We were told first to review the instructions, and then you can begin to answer the questions.

4. The professor said, "The examination will conclude in one hour", and that we had to answer all of the questions in two out of three sections.

5. After the exam was over, the professor tells us it counts for half of the final grade.

6. When a student completes the exam and puts down their pen, they often feel a great sense of relief that it is over.

7. One student works through the questions too quickly and many mistakes are made.

8. The marking of the exams is up to the teaching assistant, but they don't usually assign the final grade.

Activity 47-3

Avoiding unnecessary shifts (See 47a–e.)

Edit the following passage to avoid distracting shifts. More than one edited version is possible.

In the year 2000, the entire community of Latin American musicians received recognition for their contributions to American music. When Carlos Santana won eight Grammy awards in 2000, he reaches the pinnacle of recognition from American popular culture. Other Latin American performers such as Ricky Martin, Jennifer Lopez, and Marc Antony achieved popular acclaim in the U.S. Consequently, these performers became part of what the media calls "The Latin Invasion." Constantly hearing the music of these artists on the airwaves, music-loving Americans gobble up their records and went to their concerts in droves. One music industry spokesperson claimed, "I haven't seen anything like this since the British Invasion" and that we're still feeling its influence.

Activity 47-4

Eliminating mixed constructions (See 47f–h.)

Edit the following sentences by eliminating mixed constructions. Some sentences have more than one possible answer.

1. The outrageous exploitation of our natural resources has diminished to the point where several species are threatened or endangered.

2. The fact that spotted owls has transmitters placed on them measured their range.

3. The calculations of the study counted the owls with transmitters to learn how much territory they would need.

4. When a forest is preserved in parcels of five square miles strictly curtails the logging there.

5. The situation with extensive clear-cutting of the old-growth forest has destroyed the owl's natural habitat.

6. An old-growth forest is when trees of various ages, up to several hundred years old, and several species live together in an undisturbed way.

7. The reason old-growth forests are important is because many creatures live there that cannot survive on tree farms.

8. A tree farm is when the ancient forest is cut down and whole areas of new trees are planted.

Activity 47-5

Eliminating mixed constructions (See 47f–h.)

Edit the following passage by eliminating mixed constructions. More than one edited version is possible.

The dissatisfaction of community members often charges that important decisions are made behind closed doors, or at least doors without welcome signs. The reason is because many feel it is their right to have information ahead of time about the decisions made at town meetings. Local newspapers usually have summaries of town affairs, but some say they are never totally accurate or very thorough. By feeling that they don't have to check with members of the community before voting on every issue means the local officials are confident of their own opinions. Being an elected official is when you make certain decisions on behalf of the members of the community.

Activity 47-6

Editing for sentence consistency (See 47a-h.)

Edit the following passage, making all sentences consistent and complete. More than one edited version is possible.

I'll bet that most people sit down to their dinner between six and seven o'clock each night. You can tell because that's when the infuriating salespeople from the local paper call. He pretends that I already have a subscription, and then he'll ask you. "Was your paper delivered on time today?" or whether it was late. It is especially annoying is where they ask the same question every time. And they think that if you say, "No, I'm not a subscriber," somehow I will agree to listen to their sales pitch. What makes it even worse is a terrible newspaper. If they were trying to sell me the New York Times would be different story.

Correct Verb Use

Activity 48-1

Eliminating incorrect verb forms (See 48a-b.)

Edit the following passage to eliminate incorrect verb forms. More than one edited version is possible.

Many people think that winter is the most dangerous season for bacterial infections. But summertime can be dangerous, too. If you are careful, though, you can avoid these summertime dangers. The first place to have watched for disease-causing bacteria in the summer is the water. Generally, pools are carefully monitor. But lakes and ponds were another story. Severe stomach upset can be bringed on by bacteria such as salmonella and shigella. These bacteria may lay waiting in natural bodies of water. Be careful not to ingest water if you swam in lakes and ponds. Experts recommend that you contact the local health department if you are unsure about a particular body of water. Be careful also with food in the summer. Disease-causing bacteria such as salmonella and listeria can create problems if food were not handled properly. For example, you should not leave foods like tuna salad or potato salad setting on your kitchen counter for very long. Similarly, you should not leave foods like these laying in a hot car. Meat can have been especially dangerous. If it is froze, meat should be thawn in the refrigerator. After it is thawed, it should be cooked and ate right away.

Activity 48-2

Using standard verb forms (See 48a-b.)

Edit the following sentences using the correct -s and -ed forms and forms of irregular verbs.

1. Sheehy share experiences that focus on concerns common to all people.

2. She start as a fashion editor and then writed features for a major New York newspaper.

3. She also contribute to magazines as an editor and freelance writer before her career as a novelist begun.

4. Although her first novels receive mixed reviews, she persevere and hope to publish more novels.

5. Her novels is about common human experiences.

Activity 48-3

Using standard verb forms (See 48a-b.)

Edit the following passage, using the correct -s and -ed forms and forms of irregular verbs.

The waiter setted down two hot chocolates topped with whipped cream at the table where we sat. The bell over the door rung repeatedly as a steady stream of hungry diners enter. The winter sun shined brightly through the large glass panes next to us as we drunk our hot chocolate. I be resting comfortably in the corner of the booth when suddenly I beholded the woman at the next tble as she sprung up and walk toward the door. I gave my companion a questioning look and asked, "What do you think she meaned by that?"

Activity 48-4

Using auxiliary verbs (See 48d.)

Complete the following sentences by supplying an appropriate auxiliary verb in each blank. Some sentences may have more than one possible answer.

1. Children were taught the rudiments of education while they _____ receiving religious instruction.
2. After the home _____ destroyed by a fire around the turn of the century, Wheeler hoped that enough money _____ be raised to build a new center.
3. A new home _____ built where up to seventy children _____ reside while they waited, hoping that they _____ be adopted.
4. Around World War I, the administration provided agricultural training to the children so that they _____ grow their own food.
5. In the 1950s, the administration decided to hire social workers and psychologists who _____ further serve the children's needs.
6. The center _____ still growing today, and family therapy sessions _____ begun.

Activity 48-5

Using standard verb forms (See 48a-b.)

Using auxiliary verbs (See 48d.)

Edit the following passage, using correct verb forms.

In 1992 Amsterdam takes a bold stand to deal with the ever-increasing problem of air pollution caused by automobiles. It ban cars from its city. Following its lead, other cities has begun efforts to consider similar plans. Car-free days had occurred in Britain, France, and Italy. Some argue that the result of such events actually make a difference. For example, when the city of La Rochelle (in France) conducted its first car-free day, it report a seventy percent increase in the use of its public transportation system. After the 1998 car-free day in Britain, seventy-five percent of drivers said they be in favor of banning cars from city centers. But becoming a car-free city was not as easy as it sounds. According to J.H. Crawford, a major proponent of the car-free city, the major challenge of becoming car-free are " to remove cars and trucks from cities while at the same time improving mobility and reducing its total costs."

Activity 48-6

Understanding verb tenses (See 48e.)

Edit the following passage, changing all present-tense verbs into corresponding past-tense forms.

For several years the price of college tuition has been increasing for would be college students and their parents. These students and their parents are concerned, if not alarmed, at the cost of a college education. However, some states are finding a way to stop the increase: prepaid tuition. The leader of this prepayment movement is Virginia, which offers Virginia families the opportunity to prepay tomorrow's college tuition at today's prices. The Virginia Prepaid Education Program (VPEP) follows a simple idea. Payments are invested so that a steady growth will cover future college tuition and mandatory fees. VPEP benefits can also be applied toward the cost of tuition and fees at Virginia private colleges, as well as most colleges and universities nationwide. Plans such as VPEP help students and their parents breath easier.

Activity 48-7

Understanding verb tenses (See 48e.)

Edit the following passage twice, changing the verbs first to the present tense and then to the future tense.

For one week at the beginning of each semester sororities opened their houses to prospective members. The women took their best dresses off their hangers and carefully painted on their makeup. Along with frozen hair went frozen smiles. Hundreds of young women moved from house to house where they were looked over and judged. For some women this was an exciting time; for others it was humiliating and degrading.

Activity 48-8

Using the present tense for habitual or future actions (See 48e.)

Edit the following passage, using the literary present tense consistently.

Each week in the tutorial following the lecture we will discuss a different dialogue of Plato. This week we are discussing The Symposium. In this dialogue, which Plato wrote in the fourth century B.C., a group of Athenian men gathered at a dinner party and took turns talking about what they thought love was. One of the guests is Socrates, whose speech was actually the centerpiece of the work. The speakers who precede Socrates also contribute interesting points, including Aristophanes, who writes comedies in real life. He expressed his view that love is more than physical desire, an idea that Socrates comes back to later in the dialogue. Next week we will read Plato's Republic.

Activity 48-9

Using the simple present tense to write about literature (See 48e.)

Edit the following passage, using the simple present tense to write about literature. See example on p. 279 of *CWR*.

Billy Budd, having seen the gangway punishment, was determined that he would always perform his duties well, and that his action will not be cause even for oral reprimand. Nevertheless, Billy finds himself getting into small difficulties on occasion. Perplexed, Billy went to the Dansker, a veteran sailor who has taken a liking to Billy. After telling the old man his troubles, Billy asked for his opinion. The old man laconically replied, that Jemmy Legs (meaning the master-at arms) is "down on him." Astonished, Billy protested that Claggart always spoke pleasantly to him. To this the old man cynically replies that that

is because Claggart really disliked Billy.

Activity 48-10

Using the subjunctive mood (See 48f.)

Edit the following sentences, using subjunctive verb forms wherever appropriate. Circle the number of any correct sentence.

1. Phil wished that he was going somewhere else tonight.

2. If he had already made plans he would not have to attend.

3. He could have made other plans if he would have thought about it earlier.

4. As the door opened, Phil put a smile on his face as though he was happy to be there.

5. He would have worn a tuxedo if he had known that formal dress were required.

Activity 48-11

Using the subjunctive mood (See 48f.)

Edit the following passage, using subjunctive verb forms wherever appropriate.

He opens the refrigerator door and catches sight of the single slice of birthday cake. If only it was not the last piece of cake! A voice inside his head demands that he does not eat it. "If it is not my birthday, I should not eat the last piece of cake," he thinks. But a second voice insists that he helps himself. "If it was my birthday, I would not mind if someone else eats it," he reasons. His conscience prevails. He sighs, closes the refrigerator door, and wishes that he has never even come into the kitchen.

Activity 48-12

Using the correct verb form, tense and mood (See 48a-f.)

Edit the following passage, using the correct form, tense, and mood of each verb. More than one edited version is possible.

In the early years of this century, the Constitution stated that women cannot vote. Suffragists wished that every woman citizen was able to vote and they strived to amend the Constitution so that no state can deny any citizen the right to vote on account of sex. For this to happen, the Constitution required that three-quarters of the states were in favor of the amendment. Many of the arguments against women's suffrage strike us as absurd now. Some people argued that women do not understand the business world; others said that the cost of elections will go up. If women would get the vote, some worried, next they would want to hold office. Some felt that a woman is represented by her husband and that when he voted it was as though she was voting. Some also feared that a vote for women will be a step toward feminism, which many people consider a radical and dangerous idea.

Subject-Verb Agreement

Activity 49-1

Making subjects and verbs agree (See 49a-j.)

Edit the following passage to make subjects and verbs agree. More than one edited version is possible.

Those in favor of government funding for the arts argues that without the arts, civilizations would cease to exist. But without the sciences, civilizations would not exist in the first place. All important civilizations, from ancient China and the Roman Empire to America in the twentieth century, has acknowledged the importance of scientific research. To ignore the important advances of science are dangerous for a society. Today, the economics of scientific funding is very complex. Determining which of various research projects get funded is difficult. The number of projects receiving funding are limited by today's weak economy. Much of today's funding goes toward applied science. Included in this category is cancer research and advances in industrial technology. Millions of dollars is spent on applied scientific research each year. But the parent of applied research projects are pure science. Research on a particular plant species or experimenting with subatomic particles is an example of pure science. Data from pure scientific research forms the base on which applied research build. Many people acknowledge the importance of funding for applied research. But few recognizes how crucial pure scientific research continues to be. A new treatment for disease or an advance in computer technology never happen without the necessary groundwork in pure science. Because we can see direct results, applied science sometimes seems more important and more exciting than pure science. But neither are enough alone. International Business Machines (IBM) are important, but so are the calculations and theories of a researcher in pure mathematics.

Activity 49-2

Ignoring words between subject and verb (See 49b.)

Finding the subject when it follows the verb (See 49c.)

Finding the subject of a linking verb (See 49d.)

Edit the following sentences to make each verb agree with its subject. Take special care when identifying the subject. Circle the number of any sentence that is correct.

1. A debate, especially for a candidate who is low in the polls, matter considerably.
2. The public's perception of the candidates' performances make a huge difference in an election.
3. Students of the political process has long been fascinated by the impact of the debate on the 1960 election.
4. Richard M. Nixon and John F. Kennedy, each a respected politician, was intelligent and articulate.

5. Many political analysts believe that the debates were the deciding factor in the election.

6. There was many people who thought that Nixon looked bad on televison.

7. Others, who listened to the debates on the radio only, has said that Nixon argued more effectively.

8. During the 1992 campaign, the format of the debates were discussed at length.

9. Bill Clinton, along with the two other candidates, George Bush and Ross Perot, were on the stage three times.

10. There was questions from members of the audience in the second debate.

Activity 49-3

> **Ignoring words between subject and verb (See 49b.)**
>
> **Finding the subject when it follows the verb (See 49c.)**
>
> **Finding the subject of a linking verb (See 49d.)**
>
> Edit the following passage to make verbs agree with their subjects. Take special care when identifying the subject.

Canada, along with Europe and many cities in the United States, have found great success in curbing the spread of AIDS through needle exchange programs. These kinds of programs is an effective way to slow down the spread of the virus among intravenous drug users. There are many who are convinced that providing addicts with clean needles does not result in increased drug use. Others, who think that such programs encourage the use of drugs and sends the wrong message to young people, remains firmly opposed. To this group, free needles and free drug use is one and the same. But, supporters of the idea points out, one of the most important parts of needle exchange programs are educating users about the dangers of sharing needles. After all, intravenous drug users is a segment of the population with an especially high rate of HIV infection, which causes AIDS. And the spread of AIDS and other infectious diseases are a matter of concern for all people.

Activity 49-4

> **Making verbs agree with subjects joined by _and_ (See 49e.)**
>
> **Making verbs agree with subjects joined by _or_ or _nor_ (See 49f.)**
>
> Edit the following sentences to make verbs agree with their compound subjects. Circle the number of any sentence that is correct.

1. Neither the butler nor the chauffeur behave oddly in front of the police.

2. Each man and woman is under suspicion.

3. Not only the time of death but also the choice of weapons figure into the equation.

4. A telephone call or a message sent beyond the premises are forbidden during the investigation.

5. Motive and alibi each matters in an investigation.

6. The inspector and the coroner disagrees.

7. Neither overeating nor lack of sleep typically cause death.

8. Both strychnine and cyanide was found in the doctor's bag.

9. The sum and substance of the investigation are interrogation.

10. Not only the gardener but also the cook are a possible suspect.

Activity 49-5

Making verbs agree with collective nouns (See 49g.)

Edit each sentence, selecting the verb from the parentheses that agrees with the collective subject. Think about how the meaning changes depending on whether you select a singular or plural verb.

1. On the last day of the semester, the class usually (take/takes) the final exam.

2. The high school basketball team (have lost/has lost) most of its games.

3. This newly formed band (play/plays) oldies.

4. The committee (decide/decides) who goes on the trip.

5. The police (enjoy/enjoys) the annual picnic.

6. The Yankees usually (field/fields) a good team.

7. The British (enjoy/enjoys) soccer.

Activity 49-6

Making verbs agree with indefinite pronouns (See 49h.)

Edit the following sentences to make verbs agree with indefinite pronoun subjects. Circle the number of any sentence that is correct.

1. All of the employees thinks that the hours are too long.

2. Much of their dissatisfaction result from their low salaries and poor benefits.

3. Neither of the women executives have been promoted in ten years.

4. Of the profits earned in the last quarter, more is slated for research and development than for improving working conditions.

5. With the salary freeze, none of the clerical staff is getting more money this year.

Activity 49-7

      Making verbs agree with collective nouns (See 49g.)

      Making verbs agree with indefinite pronouns (See 49h.)

      Making verbs agree with <u>who</u>, <u>which</u>, and <u>that</u> (See 49i.)

      Edit the following subjects to make verbs agree with collective noun subjects, indefinite pronoun subjects, and relative pronoun subjects. Circle the number of any sentence that is correct.

1. The pictures in the exhibit, which are open every night, feature children from Third World countries.

2. Many of the children photographed in Mexico was casualties of the earthquake.

3. Most people find that it is the look of sadness on their faces that are most moving.

4. The best of the photographers, who spend three months every year in Southeast Asia, has won numerous awards.

5. The museum committee has a variety of opinions on the exhibit.

6. Adding photography exhibits to the museum was one of many good ideas of the curator, who is herself a photographer.

7. Much of her energy are spent finding good exhibits and soliciting contributions from patrons.

Activity 49-8

      Making verbs agree with subjects that refer to amounts (See 49j.)

      Edit the following sentences to make verbs agree with subjects that refer to amounts. Circle the number of any sentence that is correct.

1. They are especially hungry because seven hours has elapsed since their last meal.

2. Half the restaurants on this street caters to businesspeople.

3. Three-quarters of the items on the menu has meat in them.

4. Half the guests is vegetarian.

5. Ninety percent of their choices is unavailable.

6. Usually they go to restaurants where one hundred percent of the dishes is meatless.

7. A dollar and a quarter are not much to pay for a soft drink.

8. Thirty dollars are more than he expected to pay for a main course.

9. Twenty dollars are all she can afford.

10. Half her money is being saved for a taxi to take her home after dinner.

Activity 49-9

Making verbs agree with subjects that refer to amounts (See 49j.)

Using singular verbs with noun phrases or clauses (See 53b.)

Edit the following sentences to make verbs agree with their subjects that refer to amounts, noun phrase subjects, or clause subjects. Circle the number of any sentence that is correct.

1. That she might be able to help suffering animals have contributed to her decision to be a vet.

2. Immunizing cats and dogs against rabies protect humans as well as their pets.

3. Two hundred dollars are a lot to pay for a routine examination.

4. Half the cat owners in the United States believe that declawing is inhumane.

5. To care for their four-footed companions are the responsibility of all animal lovers.

Activity 49-10

Using singular verbs with noun phrases or clauses (See 53b.)

Using singular verbs with titles and words used as words (See 49j.)

Using singular verbs with singular subjects that end in -s (See 49j.)

Using singular verbs with troublesome plurals (See 49j.)

Edit the following sentences to make verbs agree with their noun phrase or noun clause subjects, subjects that are titles or words used as words, or troublesome singular or plural subjects. Circle the number of any sentence that is correct.

1. Politics are not a field that I find interesting, but I do enjoy my world literature course.

2. Dostoyevsky's *Crime and Punishment* are exactly the sort of novel I would choose to read on my own.

3. That a young man would commit a murder for the reasons Dostoyevsky describes seems unthinkable to me.

4. To make interesting contributions to the weekly class discussions are one of my goals.

5. Witticisms are what I would like my classmates to call my comments.

Activity 49-11

    Using singular verbs with titles and words used as words (See 49j.)

    Edit the following sentences to make verbs agree with their subjects. Circle the number of any sentence that is correct.

1.   Jane Smiley's Ordinary Love and Goodwill are in a display case at the front of the store.

2.   Monkeys are what the parents affectionately call their children in Susan Minot's first novel, which is also on sale.

3.   Dostoyevsky's Crime and Punishment, which explore the complex psychology of human character, is sold out.

4.   Alex Haley's Roots was made into a television miniseries.

5.   Barnes and Noble also have these titles available.

Activity 49-12

    Using singular verbs with singular subjects that end in -s (See 49j.)

    Using singular verbs with troublesome plurals (See 49j.)

    Edit the following sentences to make verbs agree with their troublesome singular and plural subjects. Circle the number of any sentence that is correct.

1.   There is no single criterion for developing an economic plan.

2.   Current data suggests that tax increases will be required to reduce the deficit.

3.   The news are not good for those who expected to pay less.

4.   Demographics are an important tool in developing a fair plan.

5.   The media describes the new plan as "strong medicine."

6.   Telecommunications are the name of the game in getting the message across.

7.   The medium of television is where most people get their news.

8.   Existing statistics indicates that spending cuts will also be necessary.

9.   Advanced mathematics are helpful in understanding the new tax schedule.

Activity 49-13

Making verbs agree with their subjects (See 48a-j.)

Edit the following passage to make verbs agree with their subjects. More than one edited version is possible.

The county employees and volunteers who run the prison education program focuses on illiteracy. Statistics shows that among prison inmates nationwide, some 60 percent is illiterate, and neither substance abuse programs nor vocational training seem as effective as literacy education in limiting the return of repeat offenders. The core of the program, therefore, are reading and writing skills. Each employee and volunteer go through a three-week training program in literacy education. If they can demonstrate sufficiently high reading levels, inmates may also train to become tutors; by doing so, most earns points toward early probation. Tutoring for all participants takes place not only one on one but also in groups, and there is within each group inmates at various levels of reading proficiency. Even inmates who have never achieved any academic success learns without feeling intimidated. Current data shows a high rate of success.

Pronoun Use

Activity 50-1

Editing for pronoun reference (See 50a.)

Edit the following passage to make all pronouns agree with their antecedents. More than one edited version is possible.

Each of us has our own oddities. One of mine is a certain fondness for cows. It started on a walk one day, when I passed a field where a herd of cows was grazing, enclosed by a split-rail fence. Each cow and calf occupied their own square of grass, a long way off from the road—all but one of them, which was right by the fence. This is my chance to see a cow close up, I thought. As I came nearer, I saw why the cow was there all alone—their head was stuck in the fence! Poor thing. If it had tried to get out, it would have kept hitting the back of its head on the top rail of the fence. It probably figured it was safer—and less painful—just to stay put. Perhaps it had been trapped for several long hours. Would it have seemed long to a cow, I wondered? I decided to try and help. I had never been this close to a cow before, let alone touched one. I was a bit skittish. Nevertheless, I took the sides of its head in my hands and gently turned them to the side, until one ear was facing the sky. Amazingly, the cow stepped backwards, pulled its head out from between the fence rails, and then just lumbered off to rejoin the herd. A dog or cat in the same predicament would have been jumping out of their skin. But this huge, powerful animal was so calm and accepting of whatever came its way, whether hindrance or help. I feel that such a spirit deserves admiration and affection. I hope that cow is still there, munching sweet grass and happily hanging out with the rest of the herd.

Activity 50-2

Making pronouns agree with antecedents joined by <u>and</u> (See 50b.)

Making pronouns agree with antecedents joined by <u>or</u> and <u>nor</u> (See 50b.)

Making pronouns agree with collective nouns (See 50b.)

Edit the following passage by making pronouns agree with their corresponding antecedents. Be especially careful about compound and collective antecedents.

Both the supervisor and her new assistant, James, are unhappy with his mutual arrangement. The supervisor admits that each regular task and special assignment is given the attention they deserve, but her assistant takes too much time to complete each one. The rest of the staff say it agrees with her. What does the assistant say in his own defense? As a junior person and a new member of the staff, he finds it difficult to handle new projects on their own and would like more help from his supervisor. He worries that someday either his irritation or his frustrations will make itself heard.

Activity 50-3

Making pronouns agree with collective nouns and indefinite nouns (See 50b.)

Edit the following sentences by selecting the correct pronoun. Be careful about the use of sexist pronouns. More than one edited version is possible.

1. One of the boy scouts has forgotten (his, their) cap.

2. Everyone complains when filling out (their, his or her) income tax forms.

3. The audience rose to (its, their) feet.

4. Aerobic exercises are good because (it, they) can strengthen the heart

5. The Smithville School Board opened (its, their) meeting to the public.

6. All the players on the girls' basketball team have forgotten (their, her) sneakers.

7. Each mother thinks (their, her) child is the most beautiful.

8. Don't misuse diet pills; (it, they) can be dangerous.

9. The company failed because no one liked (its, their) products.

10. All police officers must wear (his or her, their) badges in the courtroom.

Activity 50-4

Making pronouns agree with their antecedents (See 50a.)

Edit the following passage by making pronouns agree with their antecedents. (You may have to change some verbs and nouns as well.) More than one edited version is possible.

Changes in facial hair, a higher or lower voice, and a decreased sex drive: this is some of the side effects of taking steroids. Yet many continue in their use of this dangerous drug. Athletics is ever more competitive and athletes are always striving to be the best he or she can be. In a race, mere seconds are along time to an athlete when they mean the difference between a gold and silver medal. Perhaps the athlete does not know what harm they are doing to their bodies. There is no physical addiction to steroids; any addiction to it is psychological and based on the fact that athletes like what they see. Unfortunately, the athlete cannot always see what lies ahead for them. Ben Johnson and some others should count himself lucky. All Johnson lost was a gold medal and the chance to compete again. Benjamin Ramirez was not so lucky. Nor were the many like him who lost his life.

Activity 50-5

Clarifying pronoun reference (See 50a.)

Edit the following passage to clarify pronoun reference. More than one edited version is possible.

A small but amazing revolution has recently taken place in New York City: the transformation of Bryant Park. Once it was a drug pushers' domain that law-abiding persons were careful to avoid. Now, after long and careful renovations, it is a safe, beautiful, welcoming spot that they eagerly seek out and linger in. If you have not been there, you must make a point to go with a companion and maybe a bag lunch. They let you have your choice of seating: benches under the trees alongside gravel walkways where you can watch people stroll or jog by; folding chairs that you can pick up and move anywhere your heart desires; or the broad, beautiful central lawn, where so many others are already lying in the sun. That is one of the best things about it. I myself love to take a chair and just rest in the sweet air and the calm atmosphere created by the trees, grass, and flowers. Birds are drawn to the park, too, and I love to watch them strut, peck, and swoop, which are endlessly interesting. To watch all the people is wonderful, too. Everyone is so relaxed. People, they are sitting alone on chairs, like I am, just looking around. They are not going anywhere. They are not fighting with each other over a cab. They are not cranky and nasty and cutthroat. Some of them, which are paired up, are lying on the grass, necking passionately or just napping peacefully. If you know the midtown area of New York City at all, you know how striking all this is. This park is a great gift to them.

Activity 50-6

Making each pronoun refer to a single antecedent (See 50a.)

Edit the following passage by making each pronoun refer clearly to a single antecedent. More than one edited version is possible.

Diane spotted Laura as she was beginning her regimen of stretching exercises. It was twenty minutes before the race was due to begin. Diane told Laura that she thought she would win the race. She was just plain faster. Laura responded that she had a good chance, but that she was going to be tough to beat. Nodding in agreement, Diane shook hands with Laura. "Good luck," she said. "Have a good race."

Activity 50-7

Providing explicit antecedents (See 50a.)

Edit each of the following sentences so that all pronouns refer to explicit antecedents. Make any small changes in wording that are needed for clarity. More than one edited version is possible.

1. When I listened to the news this morning, they said the President would meet with Russian leaders next month.
2. Joan told Diane she was better off without her old boyfriend.
3. The dog across the street got into a fight with a neighbor's cat, and it had to be taken to the vet's as a result.
4. I can't stand my calculus class. She keeps giving us too much homework.
5. It's hard to find a nice apartment off campus; they charge too much for rent around here.

Activity 50-8

Providing explicit antecedents (See 50a.)

Edit the following passage by making all pronouns refer to explicit antecedents. More than one edited version is possible.

The fraternity house that I visited was not as neat inside as I had expected from knowing them. Its old and worn furniture may have made it look worse than it was, but I for one didn't feel like sitting down on any of the couches. The fraternity brothers made it sound like the best thing in the world to be a part of. Downstairs there was a huge crowd. The brothers said that most nights a long line to get food stretches out into the hall, with everybody pushing to get to the front. This is typical. The brothers wall pretty nice, but at one point in the evening they had a toast to the crowd and they threw garbage on everyone at the party, which I didn't think was too nice.

Activity 50-9

Replacing a vague it, they, or you (See 50a.)

Avoiding overuse of it (See 50a.)

Edit the following passage by clarifying all uses of the pronouns it, they, and you. Make any small changes in wording that are needed for smooth reading. More than one edited version is possible.

They say that you shouldn't believe everything you read in the newspaper. It is foolish to assume that it is possible for it to be accurate all of the time. You can't expect that there will never be a mistake. Sometimes they get late-breaking stories and have to rush to get them in before it goes to press. Occasionally you can even see contradictions between two articles on the same topic. It will say one thing in one article and then it will say something different in the other. It is when that happens that it is hard for you to know which article you should believe.

Activity 50-10

Choosing <u>who</u>, <u>which</u>, or <u>that</u> according to the antecedent (See 50a.)

Complete the following passage, filling in the blanks with the correct pronoun: <u>who</u>, <u>which</u>, or <u>that</u>.

None of the carpenters _____ I know has any use for imported nails. They swear that American-made nails are the only ones _____ are worth using. A nail _____ bends when it is driven in was probably made in Canada, they say. One box of nails, _____ they got from Japan, had heads _____ broke off if they tried to pull them out. There are problems every time the contractor brings them boxes _____ are imported. These carpenters, every one of _____ works with nails every day, believe that they can tell where a nail comes from as soon as they hit it with a hammer. One thing is certain: a bent nail doesn't get that way because a carpenter hit it crooked.

Activity 50-11

Creating clear pronoun references (See 50a.)

Edit the following passage by making sure that all pronoun references are clear and that all pronouns are used appropriately. More than one edited version is possible.

Studies have shown that alcoholism is a major problem in our city, which has a high percentage of unemployed and homeless people. This is true in other metropolitan areas as well. However, it affects not only the down-and-out but also working people, the elderly, and teenagers which have begun to experiment with drinking. We interviewed some social workers, which said that being homeless caused some people to drink. What we learned from interviewing homeless people, though, was that many of those which are homeless now, they were drinking long before they were on the street. Drink hard enough and long enough and you inevitably lose your home, it seems from their experience.

Activity 50-12

Using the correct pronoun case (See 50c.)

Edit the following passage to make sure all pronouns are in the correct case. More than one edited version is possible.

The art world is full of stories of intrigue and deception. For example in 1938 three men were hired to restore some thirteenth-century cathedral wall paintings in Schleswig, Germany. Fey, Fey, and Malskat began by cleaning all the paintings. But underneath the work of a previous restorer named Ohibers, there was practically nothing left of the paintings theirselves! The three men must have thought them to have only one option. They simply produced brand-new paintings, based on their memory of the ones they had removed during the cleaning process. These "restorations" were enchanting to whoever they were shown. Viewing they revealed surprising details about history. For instance, there were a lot of turkeys in these "restored" paintings. Scholars had believed that Europe's first turkeys were brought over from America in the sixteenth century. Now it seemed there were actually turkeys in Germany three hundred years before Columbus had even landed in America! Perhaps there had been trade between the two worlds at that early date. But this seemed unlikely. Finally, Ohibers made a statement to this effect:In my day, us restorers would always add something of our own anywhere in a painting that was blank or impossible to make out. He had, very innocently, painted a couple of turkeys. Fey, Fey, and Malskat had just added many more. Ohlbers and them had simply made a chain of honest mistakes. Twenty years and many acclaimed "restorations" later the full truth came out. Malskat was in fact a talented forger, and the Feys were his partners in crime. Whom blew the whistle? Malskat hisself did, because of an unsettled score between he and the Feys. The Feys had gotten far more glory, credit, and pay for their work than him. Malskat wanted his own fair share. What he got was a prison sentence.

Activity 50-13

Choosing case for compound elements (See 50c.)

Edit the following sentences, selecting the appropriate pronoun case for compound subjects and objects.

1. Before we left on vacation, Eric and (I, me) turned off the refrigerator and locked the windows.
2. (He, Him) and (me, I) were driving to the party when we got a flat tire.
3. Carla leaned over during the test and whispered to Scott and (I, me).
4. Lisa is the pretty girl who sits in front of Matt and (I, me) in English class.
5. Just between you and (I, me), this is the hardest course I've ever taken.

Activity 50-14

Choosing case for appositive pronouns (See 50c.)

Edit the following sentences, using the appropriate case for appositive pronouns.

1. All three hikers—him, her and me—had expected the colored marks on the trees to lead us back to the head of the trail.
2. Fallen trees along the path prevented even the most determined hikers—Sarah and I—from following the trail.
3. The optimists among us, Christopher and me, knew we would eventually find our way out of the woods.
4. When the ordeal was over, the more experienced members told the three thankful hikers—Christopher, Sarah, and I—that they had been worried about us.
5. The most enthusiastic members of the expedition, Sarah and me, were ready to go back into the woods the next day.

Activity 50-15

Choosing between <u>us</u> and <u>we</u> before a noun (See 50c.)

Edit the following sentences, using <u>us</u> and <u>we</u> correctly.

1. Us reporters took notes on the relief plan as the president spoke.

2. Officials who spoke off the record gave we media people the impression that the operation would not last long.

3. They told we members of the press that the president wanted to improve conditions for the suffering people.

4. Us feature writers plan to concentrate on the humanitarian efforts of the administration.

5. The president told we newswriters that he hoped that other countries would also participate.

Activity 50-16

Choosing case for compound elements (See 50c.)

Choosing case for appositive pronouns (See 50c.)

Choosing between <u>us</u> and <u>we</u> before a noun (See 50c.)

Edit the following paragraph, using the appropriate pronoun cases. Watch out for pronouns in compound subjects and objects, pronouns used as appositives, and <u>us</u> and <u>we</u> before nouns.

Fishing with our dad, Charley and me hadn't caught any fish all week. We decided it was up to the two of us, him and I, to find some way to catch something. Us two kids borrowes a rowboat and, with him and me rowing, went way out in the middle of the pond. We dropped anchor and began fishing, him out of one side of the boat and I out of the other side. Charley asked me if I was sleepy and I said, "Not me," but then a splash of water woke me, and the boat was rocking. Charley was pulling madly on his rod, and it seemed as if his catch would tip the boat over and he and I with it. It took ten minutes for us, Charley and I, to get that catfish on board. Dad said it was turning out that the real fishers in the family were Charley and me. Dad made both Charley and I feel really proud.

Activity 50-17

Choosing case with verbals (See 50c.)

Edit the following sentences, using the correct pronoun case with verbals. Some sentences have more than one possible answer.

1. George looked positively stunned by us yelling "Surprise!" when he opened the door.

2. It was amusing for we to watch his unwrapping the gifts that we brought.

3. As we waited for George to cut the cake, it seemed to us that him thanking everyone for the gifts was taking forever.

4. We all sang "Happy Birthday" and watched his blowing out the candles.

5. The occasion called for him eating the biggest piece of cake.

Activity 50-18

Choosing case after <u>than</u> or <u>as</u> (See 50c.)

Edit the following sentences, using the correct pronoun case after <u>than</u> and <u>as</u>. Circle the number of any sentence that is correct.

1. I consider myself just as good an announcer had her.

2. Me playing the latest hits has contributed to my success.

3. Surveys show that her programs appeal to a wider audience than me.

4. The other station in town would like we to be less popular.

5. We give out more free tickets to performances than them.

6. One thing is for sure: we don't play as much dull music as they.

Activity 50-19

Choosing between <u>who</u> and <u>whom</u> (See 50c.)

Edit the following passage, using <u>who</u>, <u>whom</u>, <u>whoever</u>, and <u>whomever</u> correctly.

Whomever was it who said that the shortest distance between two points is a straight line? I don't know, but it was certainly someone wise. This maxim implies directness, and anybody whom is trying to write effectively should keep these words in mind. Karen Branch, who is featured regularly in my favorite magazine, knows how to be direct and get to the point. Right at the start, Branch makes the content of an article perfectly clear to whomever is reading it. By avoiding rambling musings and cute anecdotes she gives to the reader who she is addressing only the facts—the what, where, when, how, and whom. Everyone who reads her articles, whomever they are, admires her for her integrity.

Activity 50-20

Using reflexive pronouns as objects (See 50c.)

Edit the following sentences, using the correct reflexive pronoun. Circle the number of any sentence that is correct.

1. My friend Mark tells stories as much to amuse him as the rest of us.

2. According to my friends and myself, there's no better place to swap stories than the neighborhood coffeehouse.

3. My friends and myself often laugh among ourselves when we recall our favorite tales from high school.

4. Sometimes when we get going, we tell ourselves not to be so noisy, and sometimes the coffeehouse owner tells us the same.

5. If you were to ask my friends and myself what word best describes ourselves, we would say "comrades."

Activity 50-21 (See 50c.)

Using appropriate the pronoun case (See 50c.)

Edit the following passage, using the appropriate pronoun cases throughout.

In the memories of my siblings and myself, our house used to be surrounded by a forest on three sides. Us children—my three brothers and me—used to hunt for snakes and salamanders in the woods by overturning the rocks that they lived under. One of the best hunting rounds for ourselves was the land to the south of our yard. When I was eight years old, I saw a garter snake catch a frog and devour it whole. It eating the frog upset my brothers and I terribly. Us, with our childish minds, thought that snakes were nasty, cruel creatures and that frogs were clearly nicer than them. Now that I am grown up, I realize that the snake eating the frog was not an act of cruelty. Snakes eat frogs to survive just as frogs eat insects. Each creature on earth lives and dies according to the natural order of things.

Activity 50-22

Using appropriate the pronoun case (See 50c.)

Edit the following passage, using correct pronoun cases.

John, who we all thought of as an outstanding student, was almost expelled last semester. His friend Dave and him were considered the two strongest scholars in the department. Whatever intellectual debate us all engaged in—whether inside the classroom or out—those two always seemed to win the argument. Then John started spending less time on his studies and more time with a group of people who he referred to only as "The Brothers."

John once said, "Us students have to hit the books week after week if we really want to excel. You're only as good as your last paper." But now he spent all his time with his new friends, and none of us challenged him wasting his days with them. Whomever knew about it just kept quiet. As for myself, I never asked him why I saw him at the library so infrequently. I guess we all figured it was something he would work out for himself. None of us were happy with him failing class after class. But by the end of the semester, the damage was done.

Adjectives and Adverbs

Activity 51-1

Using adjectives and adverbs correctly (See 51a-d.)

Edit the following passage, using adjectives and adverbs correctly. More than one edited version is possible.

More and more people are becoming aware that Alzheimer's disease is a real serious problem for our society. Not hardly anyone will go through life without knowing someone with this disease. In the United States, as many as two million people over the age of sixty-five may have Alzheimer's disease. It is even more commoner among people over the age of eighty. Alzheimer's disease is one of the most common and least understood diseases known today. Researchers have identified two different types of Alzheimer's disease. The first type occurs in people over sixty-five and develops more slowly. In the second type, which occurs in people under sixty-five, the symptoms of the disease develop most quickly. People with Alzheimer's disease usually go through several different stages. In the early stages of the disease, patients often seem quite healthily. But by the time they reach the latter stages, most Alzheimer's patients can no longer care for themselves. In the final stages of the disease, many patients simply lie curled up in bed. The family members of people with Alzheimer's disease sometimes feel badly and blame themselves. But the disease is no one's fault. Doctors have not identified one most absolute cause of Alzheimer's disease. But research into the disease continues, and doctors hope that one day less people will have to suffer with this disease.

Activity 51-2

Choosing adjectives or adverbs (See 51a.)

Edit the following sentences, using an adjective or an adverb when each is needed.

1. Measuring correct is the most important part of woodworking.

2. You have to measure real carefully, but your care is likely to pay off in the end.

3. For fine work, measure close. Use a pencil that marks clean.

4. Then you have to cut straight and true. Leave just a part of your mark showing, and the piece should fit perfect.

5. Any good woodworker can give you handily suggestions like these.

Activity 51-3

Using adjectives after linking verbs (See 51b.)

Edit the following sentences, using adjectives and adverbs correctly after linking verbs. Circle the number of any sentence that is correct.

1. Most Hitchcock thrillers seem odd humorous to the moviegoer.
2. Viewers become preparedly to witness horrific acts once they realize that dark humor usual precedes violence.
3. Do they feel positively or negatively about this subtle manipulation?
4. In the theatre, their faces appear really anxiously, and their laughter sounds nervous.
5. But when they leave the theatre, feel strangely excitedly by the experience.

Activity 51-4

Choosing between commonly confused modifiers (See 51c.)

Avoiding double negatives (See 51e.)

Edit the following passage, using the correct form of any commonly confused modifier and correcting any double negatives.

Things have been going real bad for the homeless in recent weeks. First, the city shut its main shelter. Later, a charity soup kitchen ran out of money. Every year the city seems to have more needy people and less dollars to help them. A more comprehensive program would mean less women and children sleeping on the street. Many of these people cannot hardly read or write good enough to get a job that pays good. With only a shelter to live in it's hard for them to feel well about themselves. They eat bad and they sleep bad, so it isn't no wonder tht they feel bad too.

Activity 51-5

Avoiding double negatives (See 51e.)

Edit the following sentences, eliminating any double negatives. Some sentences can be edited in more than one way. Circle the number of any sentence that is correct.

1. They don't have no idea of the side effects of anabolic steroids. About the many dangers of these powerful drugs they haven't heard nothing.
2. No matter what athletes may want to believe, it just isn't true that steroids cause no physical problems.
3. It's not as if don't have no psychological effects either.

4. There are hardly no parts of the body that can't be affected in one way or another.

5. It doesn't make no sense for the family members of athletes to ignore the warning signs of steroid use.

Activity 51-6

Using comparatives and superlatives correctly (See 51a.)

Edit the following sentences, using comparatives and superlatives correctly. Some sentences can be edited in more than one way. Circle the number of any sentence that is correct.

1. Computers can do many things, but the amazingest thing they can do is connect you with huge banks of data.

2. With an on-line data service you can make more better use of your computer.

3. Compared to browsing in a library, using an on-line data service is usually the best choice.

4. For finding baseball statistics, Supreme Court opinions, and medical journal articles, a service is more effective.

5. The most fastest way to research a subject is to search books, newspapers, and magazine articles for keywords.

6. For example, you could use "Control Data Corp." and "stock" as keywords to find out why the company's stock was doing more bad this year than last year.

7. A most unique on-line service is offered by some libraries.

8. The most quickest way to call up the card catalog is with your home computer.

9. Of course, you can waste time browsing, but having no access at all seems like the worser choice.

10. You'll have more better access to the information by using a computer, and in less time.

Activity 51-7

Using comparatives and superlatives correctly (See 51d.)

Edit the following passage, using the correct comparative and superlative forms of adjectives and adverbs. More than one edited version is possible.

School violence has been increasing more steadlier over the past decade in the United States. High-profile school shootings have forced us to take more closer look at not only the causes of such behavior but also preventative measures in order to better protect our nation's youth. More oftener than not, those students who commit the violence have been victims of bullying during school. Taking a proactive stance, schools are offering coping classes to students on how to deal with bullies. These classes will help our youth recognize potentially violent situations and the bestest techniques to stop bullying before it escalates. With this new proactive approach, perhaps students who have been bullied will find that going to school can be less scarier and eventually more safer.

Activity 51-8

Using adjectives and adverbs correctly (See 51a-e.)

Edit the following passage, using adjectives and adverbs correctly. More than one edited version is possible.

The fall leaves that had looked so colorfully had turned a more duller color and fallen from the trees weeks ago, leaving the woods grayer and more lonelier. The most sharpest, bitterest wind blew against me as I walked down the dirt road. I had to admit that I was likely to feel badly tomorrow. My hands felt warmly inside my woolen gloves, but I didn't have no hat. My ears felt raw, and the inside of my head throbbed bad.

I felt happier when I saw the large red building with its well-maintained outbuildings. The air smelled pungently: manure, feed, and animal smells were mixed together indistinguishable. I went over to the horse stalls in the barn, where real fragrant wood chips covered the dirt floor, strewn there to absorb the odors of the barn. The horses, covered up good in their colorful blankets seemed peaceful in their stalls. The warm air felt heavenly and, exhaustedly, I unzipped my jacket and sat down on the floor. I didn't know of no better place to get off my feet and rest for a while.

Modifier Placement

Activity 52-1

Eliminating misplaced modifiers (See 52a-d.)

Edit the following passage to eliminate incorrectly placed modifiers. More than one edited version is possible.

One of the reasons I love swimming is that it makes me feel just strong. The farther I get into my thirty-six laps, the tougher I feel. Instead of spending my energy, it's being multiplied. The thoughts that go through my mind, even though I know this is just the effect of endorphins, are fabulous. Normally, I mean, my body image is something like this:I'm a wreck. But in the pool, I become the greatest undiscovered athlete of the decade—maybe even of the century. My body is uniquely and perfectly designed to execute this sport! People are moving over to the slow lane because they want to stay out of my way! Then another thing I love abut swimming kicks in—my mind is completely free to willy-nilly follow these trains of thought wherever they lead. I can engage in daydreaming completely guilt-free. The two people standing at the end of the pool become the swim coaches. They are admiring my endurance and the efficiency of my stroke. Soon they are going to come over and recruit me for their team. They are Olympic talent-scouting coaches better yet. WhenI tell them the only time I hae swum competitively was in the third grade, they refuse to believe me. "It just isn't possible," they say. I leave these fantasies in my gym bag, nearly always with my goggles and swimsuit. But I have a great time while I am inside them.

Activity 52-2

Repositioning misplaced modifiers (See 52a.)

Edit the following passage, moving any misplaced modifiers. More than one edited version is possible.

Most people assume that black bears hibernate all winter incorrectly. During the winter, although sleeping deeply, a true state of hibernation is not achieved by black bears. Their body temperature only drops a little, and one can wake up just a black bear with a little effort. Preparing to sleep for several months, a very large amount of food is eaten by the bears. This way, they can store fat and feed off it all winter while they are sleeping. The female surprisingly gives birth to her young at this time.

Activity 52-3

Repositioning misplaced modifiers (See 52a.)

Edit the following sentences, making sure that all modifiers are correctly placed. More than one version is possible.

1. We decided to send our daughter to college on the day she was born.

2. From that day on, we set aside a little money every month diligently.

3. Entering her senior year, we traveled to the different campuses in our mini-van.

4. Being in the van, sometimes for several hours, our conversations explored pros and cons of each college.

5. Finally, our daughter made her decision, and the day approached for us to say good-bye quickly.

6. Seeing the look of excitement and trepidation on her face as she drove off, one thought entered our mind: we made a good decision on the day she was born.

Activity 52-4

Placing limiting modifiers carefully (See 52a.)

Edit the following passage to correct the placement of limiting modifiers. More than one edited version is possible.

Some students only attend college as a way to get a good job. They understand the connection that lies between education and earning potential perfectly. They don't see that there are simply other reasons to go to college. A handful seem just to think that learning for its own sake is enough. Most don't even see that one year spent at college will enrich their lives. Imagine what just four can do!

Activity 52-5

Placing limiting modifiers carefully (See 52a.)

Edit the following sentences to correct the placement of limiting modifiers. Circle the number of any sentence that is correct.

1. She knows only how hard it is for me to be there on time. No one else does.

2. I understand that my walking in late bothers the others perfectly.

3. My bus merely runs every fifty minutes after 8:00 A.M.

4. I cannot simply make an earlier bus.

5. Why can't buses just run a bit more often?

Activity 52-6

Clarifying squinting modifiers (See 52b.)

Edit the following sentences to connect the placement of squinting modifiers. Some sentences can be edited in more than one way. Circle the number of any sentence that is correct.

1. The newspaper that they read daily has an easy puzzle.

2. The Sunday paper's puzzle is more fun for them both because it is more challenging.

3. The words that are left blank invariably are extremely obscure.

4. The dictionary that they consult rarely is helpful.

5. The puzzles that they complete usually have no errors.

Activity 52-7

Clarifying squinting modifiers (See 52b.)

Edit the following passage, correcting any squinting modifiers. More than one version is possible.

Two of us who commute between Washington and New York regularly meet for breakfast on the train. The train that we take usually makes no local stops. Menus that are handed out occasionally feature daily specials. Large mugs are given to us both for coffee and for tea. The bagel that I order always is still warm when I eat it. The jostling motion that the train makes frequently cause our drinks to spill.

Activity 52-8

Eliminating dangling modifiers (See 52c.)

Edit the following passage, clarifying squinting modifiers and eliminating dangling modifiers. More than one edited version is possible.

Examining the patient death rates of more than fifty doctors, the results were compared by a panel to a statistical average. Having a better than average rate, a minus score was entered for those doctors. A positive score was entered for those who had worse than average rates. Consisting of only the doctors with positive scores, the panel released a list of names to a local newspaper. After reading the article, a protest was lodged by the county medical society. Doctors who criticized the study strongly argued that the scoring was biased.

Activity 52-9

Eliminating dangling modifiers (See 52c.)

Edit the following sentences to eliminate any dangling modifiers. Some sentences can be edited in more than one way. Circle the number of any sentence that is correct.

1. Suffering hundreds of thousands of casualties, the armies of the Union experienced great hardships.

2. After putting an end to slavery and the agrarian way of life in the South, northern industry prospered.

3. Causing unprecedented death and destruction, more than 600,000 people died in the war.

4. Based on the plantation system, the South saw its economy change after the war.

5. Fighting for opposite causes, independence was sought by the South and restoration of the Union was desired by the North.

6. Having irreconcilable political differences, the conflict focused on whether slavery should be allowed in the new western states.

7. Having been granted the authority by Congress, over half a million men were recruited by Lincoln.

8. Having seceded from the Union, Jefferson Davis was elected provisional president of the Confederate states.

9. As the world's major cotton exporter, financial support was expected from abroad by the South.

10. Staying neutral in the conflict, there was no assistance from Britain and France.

Activity 52-10

Moving disruptive modifiers (See 52d.)

Edit the following passage, moving disruptive modifiers for easier reading. More than one edited version is possible.

The writers and editors at The New Yorker use specific tactics to effectively fire their information at a very specific audience—educated middle- and upper-class individuals who work and play in New York City. The authors attempt through skillful use of sophisticated vocabulary, varied and complex sentence structure, and stimulating content to capture this readership. Their methods have in almost all instances given the readers what they want, namely the greatest amount of information in the fewest number of words. The magazine has been able to very easily fill, in the world of the written word, a niche. Its pages can be said to be brimming with well-documented material. It has become, for its comments regarding world issues, hints on the latest happenings in the Big Apple, and lighthearted quips, well regarded.

Activity 52-11

Moving disruptive modifiers (See 52d.)

Edit the following sentences, moving disruptive modifiers for easier reading. Some sentences can be edited in more than one way. Circle the number of any sentence that is correct.

1. His books are the result of many years spent collecting data for a management consulting firm.

2. His approach is to factually relay his information.

3. His ability to thoroughly research and interview is topped only by his ability to logically organize the story line.

4. In The One-Minute Manager, Peters makes the point that, by selecting a qualified staff, a manager is able to significantly reduce his or her workload.

5. When subordinates have been properly and carefully, so that their work speaks for itself, chosen, there is no need to constantly review their work.

6. If a manager trusted their ability enough to hire them, now he or she should trust their ability to successfully produce results.

7. Peters has, with his sharp mind, managed to effectively distill the fundamental attributes of excellence down to eight major points.

8. Some people have criticized Peter's approach as too simplistic because he limits the analysis of business organizations to only eight dimensions.

9. The foundation of The Search for Excellence is the research efforts that Peters over the past twenty-five years for a management consulting firm conducted.

10. His second book, A Passion for Excellence, was able in its first four weeks on the bookstore shelves to realize sales of over 250,000.

Activity 52-12

Eliminating dangling, disruptive and squinting modifiers (See 52a-d.)

Edit the following passage, eliminating dangling, disruptive, and squinting modifiers. More than one edited version is possible.

Striking millions of Americans, some people only are afflicted by insomnia occasionally, while other people live with it for several years. Having experienced mild, occasional sleeplessness, your insomnia shouldn't be considered a major concern. The causes from which it seem most often are quite simple. Having something troubling or exciting on your mind, exerting too much physical or mental activity before bedtime, having a mild fever, drinking too much caffeine, or eating a heavy meal, sleeplessness might occur. Changing your schedule or surroundings, insomnia can also result. The way to best ensure a good night's sleep is to consistently follow a few simple steps. Try to go to bed at the same time every night. Sleep on a comfortable bed in a dark room. Realizing that it is still, after twenty minutes, hard to fall asleep, it is helpful for you to get up and do something, such as read, until you feel drowsy. And remember to always avoid caffeine and heavy foods as well as strenuous activity before bedtime.